TALENTPRENEURSHIP

HOW TO BUILD AND GROW A HEALTHY BUSINESS, TRANSFORM THE PEOPLE AROUND YOU, AND LIVE THE LIFE OF YOUR DREAMS

TALENTPRENEURSHIP

HOW TO BUILD AND GROW A HEALTHY BUSINESS, TRANSFORM THE PEOPLE AROUND YOU, AND LIVE THE LIFE OF YOUR DREAMS

BY SUNNY KAILA

FOREWORD BY JOHN C. MAXWELL

ethos
collective

Published by Ethos Collective™
PO Box 43, Powell, OH 43065
www.ethoscollective.vip

LCCN: 2023914665
Paperback ISBN: 978-1-63680-193-3
Hardcover ISBN: 978-1-63680-194-0
e-book ISBN: 978-1-63680-195-7

Available in paperback, hardcover, e-book, and audiobook

For special bonus content associated
with this book, visit Talentprenuership.net or
scan the QR code below.

Table of Contents

Dedication xi

Foreword xiii

An Invitation to Talentpreneurship™ xvii

Chapter 1: Are You Losing the Talent War? 1
    Are You and Your Business Winning
        or Losing the Talent War? 1
    The Power of People 3
    Protecting Your Brand. 6
    Professional Pain Points 7
    Leadership and Cultivating Talent 9
    Turning the Tide Toward Talent. 11

Chapter 2: My American Dream –
Taxi to Talentpreneurship. 14
    From Pumping Gas to Serving MSPs. 14
    From Farmlands to Foreign Lands 15
    The Keys to the College 18
    From Taxi to Tech. 22
    Find What Makes You Unique and Build on It 26
    Lady Liberty and the American Dream 29

Chapter 3: Staffing Up in a Post-Pandemic World 31

In the Room vs. On Zoom 32

Do Your People Measure Up? 37

The Entitlement Mindset 37

Where in the World Are Your People? 39

Staffing Up for Success 43

Where Do We Go from Here? 44

Chapter 4: What Does Your Business Really Need? . . . 46

The Goldilocks Model 47

The Sticky Wicket 49

Different Industries, Different Needs 50

Unlocking the Secrets of Talent Marketing 52

How to Lead in a Hybrid and Diverse World 53

The Challenge Ahead 56

**Chapter 5: Talent Operating System – A Framework
for Building and Sustaining Top-Talent Teams** 57

Business and Team Success…It Really Can Happen . . 57

TOS: A Blueprint for Business and Team Success . . . 59

The TOS Framework 59

Chapter 6: Entrepreneurial Success Through TOS . . . 66

Great Entrepreneurs Are Talentpreneurs First 66

The Foundation of TOS: Culture 67

It Takes a Village: Great Talentpreneurs
Build Healthy Communities 69

Every Truly Effective Community Has a
Well-Defined Purpose 70

From Vision to Victory: Talentpreneurs
Are Great Visionaries 70

The Power of Alignment: Vision, Strategy,
Goals, and Scorecards 71

Talent Acquisition 74

Chapter 7: Building an Unstoppable Team 77

Be a Superhero and Think like an Entrepreneur. . . . 77

Aligning Your Team's Strengths
with the Company's Vision. 77

Your Own Team of Superheroes 79

A Cascade of Happiness and Results 81

What Is the Cost of Happiness? 82

Encouraging Entrepreneurial Thinking
with Everyone on Your Team 85

Cut Through the Red Tape. 86

Everything Starts with Education. 88

Tools of the Trade 90

Failing Upwards 91

Entrepreneurship and Innovation 92

**Chapter 8: Employee Experience Blueprint – Cultivating
Engagement, Productivity, and Retention** 94

Employee Experience Strategies 95

Great Engagement Requires Complete Care,
Connection, and Collaboration. 96

Life By Design, NOT By Default. 96

The Program Structure 100

Implementing Life by Design 101

Great Engagement Requires Great
Communication 104

Your Opportunity in Communication. 105

Our Business Is to Be HAPPY 108

Small Talk, Big Impact 110

The Elements of Good Communication 113

Cultivate Your Garden 114

Chapter 9: The MrBeast Factor – What Millennials and Gen Zs Really Need 117
    Teenage Wasteland 119
    What We Have Here Is a Failure
        to Communicate. 121
    The Kids Are All Right 123
    Everything Is Accelerating 125
Chapter 10: The Result – Self-Managed and Profitable Business While Transforming Lives— Including Your Own 126
    360-Degree Perspective. 128
    Top Talent Retention .129
    More Than Numbers .131
    Customer Experience at Its Best. 132
    Community at Work. .133
Chapter 11: Should We Continue the Conversation? . . .135
    Transform Your Talent with Team GPS 136
    Delivering World-Class Talent for Your Team 137
    Build IT Technical and Leadership Training 139
    Final Thoughts on the Journey Ahead 140

Notes 143
Acknowledgments. 147
About Sunny Kaila 149

Dedication

This book is lovingly dedicated to my extraordinary wife, Kam Kaila, my devoted parents, Dalbir Singh and Manjit Kaur Kaila, and my three boys, Sahib, Rohan, and Shaan.

To Kam, your unwavering love, constant support, and ceaseless faith have enriched my journey in ways that words can scarcely capture. You have walked with me every step of the way, hand in hand, turning aspirations into reality. No Kam, no American Dream!

To my parents, your faith in me has been the sturdy foundation upon which I have built my dreams. Your guidance and unwavering support made my journey to America possible, nurturing in me the courage and determination to pursue my Life By Design.

To my boys, your youthfulness and inquisitive nature keep me looking at the world with a child's eyes, reminding me how awesome life can be—and should be—every day.

I also wish to express my sincerest gratitude to the IT By Design team for helping to make this dream a reality. It takes a village!

Foreword

Talent is important, but it's never enough. Years ago, I wrote a book with that exact title: *Talent Is Never Enough.* I saw a trend in sports, church, business, and organizations where people thought if you hired talent, your team would win. But talent alone will never ensure victory.

We've all seen a leader who has talent, and that's all. Although people might serve with that person for a short time, they'll leave very quickly. Talent requires character. Talent requires teamwork. Talent requires integrity.

My friend Sunny Kaila knows this better than most. He was born into a country without much opportunity. He was also born with talent. Thankfully, he had much more than talent; he had skills like self-discipline, focus preparation, belief, and perseverance.

I often say leadership is influence, nothing more, nothing less. What I like about *Talentpreneurship*™ is that Sunny goes beyond just talking about talent. He shows you how to create a talent operating system. You will understand how to attract, engage, and retain talented people. The result will be a customer experience that exceeds expectations and produces remarkable results.

The companies that succeed will be the ones who understand how to leverage talent to create more value for their clients. These companies will transform the leader and the team. It all starts with the leader who models the way, and when they do, they begin to influence the entire organization. It is a must-read!

—John C. Maxwell
New York Times Bestselling Author

Jindgi Ch Passae Kamunae Saukhe,
Bande Kamuane Akuhe

It's easier to earn money in life than to earn
people's respect and loyalty.

—Punjabi proverb, taught to me by my father.

An Invitation to Talentpreneurship™

You run a small to mid-size business (SMB), you've created more work than you can fulfill yourself, and you've hired a team to get the work done. You dream of financial independence, freedom, and a succession plan, maybe getting to an exit—selling the business and making a significant profit. There's just one problem—the people you hire are quitting halfway through projects, leaving you to scramble to get the work finished. Or your team members aren't as motivated as you need them to be. Maybe they're doing "bare minimum Mondays" or "quiet quitting" in the parlance of the day—they're showing up but barely getting their work done, and nothing you can say or do gets them engaged.

You're working longer hours than ever, you're unhappy with your team, your spouse never sees you, and work seems like a nightmare. Getting to an exit? It seems impossible.

If you relate to any of this, you aren't alone. These issues are affecting—even crippling—more SMBs than anyone can imagine. These businesses, and perhaps yours, are losing what I call Talent Wars.

This book is devoted to mastering the creation, development, and alignment of top-talent teams, which stands as the paramount element in any business. Its purpose is to guide you toward achieving exceptional levels of happiness, effectiveness, engagement, and commitment that surpass your expectations. I refer to this approach as Talentpreneurship™. By embracing Talentpreneurship, you will not only unlock the secrets to business growth and profitability, but you'll also discover the means to leading a fulfilling and healthy life along the way.

Throughout my entrepreneurial journey, transitioning from driving a cab to leading a high-growth technology organization, I acquired invaluable insights that I now term "Talentpreneurship." At the heart of achieving the American dream is my superpower: the capability to assemble high-caliber teams. This ability was instilled by my father, who emphasized the significance of surrounding oneself with exceptional individuals and consistently offering them value through Relationships, Collaboration, and Teamwork.

In this book, I draw upon my personal experience of overcoming the Talent Wars in my own business, as well as helping thousands of SMBs win those wars. The ideas, talent frameworks, processes, and best practices I share with my customers are at the heart of this book. By implementing these strategies, you can bid farewell to talent challenges, sleepless nights, missed family occasions, and the resulting strain on your relationships. Instead, you'll cultivate a devoted workforce that remains loyal and engaged, eliminating the notion of quiet quitting altogether. Your customers will experience unprecedented satisfaction as projects are completed flawlessly the first time, without interruptions or changes in team members. Day by day, the dream of achieving your dream business and exiting gracefully, with a secure succession plan in place, will become increasingly tangible.

At the heart of every remarkable business lies a visionary Talentpreneur. A Talentpreneur is an entrepreneur who achieves business success by building and retaining top-talent teams—focusing on talent first. By placing an unwavering emphasis on talent, a Talentpreneur sets the stage for unparalleled success and growth. With a keen eye for recognizing and harnessing exceptional abilities, a Talentpreneur paves the way for a thriving business that operates seamlessly and achieves remarkable milestones. Embrace your inner Talentpreneur and unlock the limitless potential that lies within your entrepreneurial journey.

1

Are You Losing the Talent War?

Are You and Your Business Winning or Losing the Talent War?

The post-COVID era has seen a major shift in business culture. The pandemic and quarantines forced many businesses, including small to mid-size businesses (SMBs), to adapt and implement work-from-home models. And now, with inflation rising and a recession looming, employees are becoming increasingly discerning about who they work for, increasing pressure on employers who are already contending with a shortage of workers with key skills. *Forbes, Fortune,* and LinkedIn have all weighed in on the importance of winning the talent war.[1]

CEO Digital has said that attracting and retaining talent will be *the* dividing line between successful and unsuccessful businesses in 2023.[2] The proliferation of communication technologies and the rise in social media platforms also means that people are more connected than ever. Job seekers are more connected to potential employers, but also customers and customers are more connected to businesses—both of which are critical elements of success. To thrive in this new era of business, you require not only excellent talent but also satisfied customers who will support and promote your product or service through online reviews and testimonials. Having the right people supporting your business is crucial to remain competitive in today's market.

Talent Wars have intensified in recent years as organizations in the United States compete for skilled workers in a competitive labor market. According to a survey by the Society for Human Resource Management (SHRM), 80 percent of HR professionals reported difficulties in recruiting suitable candidates in 2022.[3] The tech industry, in particular, has been a battleground for talent, with companies fiercely competing to attract top cloud engineers, cybersecurity experts, automation engineers, software developers, data scientists, and cybersecurity experts, and now AI prompt engineers. Stories have emerged of bidding wars between tech giants, offering extravagant compensation packages and perks to lure coveted talent. This has forced organizations to implement creative recruitment strategies and incentives to attract and retain qualified professionals.

By their very nature, SMBs are built on people. The expertise, dedication, and innovative capacity of your employees are among the greatest assets and advantages your company can have. This is especially true for technology companies. Ramsey Sahyoun, co-founder at Evergreen Services Group, a family of leading managed IT services companies, asserts that to build a great company, you have to attract the best people. Don't view "people vs. business" as a big tradeoff decision. Embrace the idea that your people are going to be the drivers of your success. If you lose the talent war, your business will falter and fail. If you do not get the people component right, it doesn't matter how good your product or technology might be—your company simply cannot succeed without the best and brightest. And no matter how great your company culture or how great the new cappuccino machine is at your open plan office, if no one is coming into that office, it's a moot point. Simply put, there is not enough talent out there to serve all businesses, even in an era of significant layoffs. Employees are sometimes even *excited* to lose their jobs because there are ten other jobs they can get instead! It can be a humbling thing for an employer to realize but knowledge is power.

As the founder and CEO of IT By Design and a thought leader on talent, I have witnessed first-hand how essential your success in the talent war is to the success of your business—and every business. Kelly Knight, the Integrator™ at EOS® Worldwide, said, "People first. Always. With great human and right-fit talent, all things are possible. If you get the people component right, the rest of the issues take care of themselves."

Talentpreneurship is all about how to attract, engage, retain, develop, and align top talent. In today's fast-changing and hyper-competitive world, winning the talent war is the key to success. In this book, I will be your guide to developing a robust talent strategy that will help you emerge victorious in this battle for talent.

So, why exactly is it so critical to win the talent war to ensure the success of your business?

The Power of People

The majority of SMBs, especially technology service companies, are essentially selling their expertise; their product, in many ways, is their people's capability. It is people who build processes, it is people who build value offerings—service offerings that you can sell. It is people who will deploy technology in your business and your customer's business to deliver services. So, with that in mind, for any business to do well, you must make sure that you have people, processes, and technology.

But people are the most important part of that equation because they are the ones building the other elements of your business. Operational maturity and efficiency are the direct result of the people who built it for you. It was Henry Ford who said, "You can take my factories, burn up my buildings, but give me my people and I'll build the business right back again." And as Jen Zaroski, VP of Human Resources at VC3, a Managed IT, and Cybersecurity Service Provider, explains, we need to remember that the people are the most crucial aspect. While data, tools, and other elements are important, our people are the most valuable resource. And without them, we're nothing. So, we need to make sure that we're working with them and treating them right.

A strong people strategy essentially means that your business is investing in people's expertise, either by paying employee salaries or consultant fees, at an X-rate per hour. Subsequently, you offer that expertise to your customers at a Y rate. The profit margin is the difference between these two values.

For instance, let's consider a scenario where you establish a cloud-building practice, and you hire a cloud engineer who earns fifty dollars per hour. To ensure profitability, you can calculate what to charge your customers on a recurring monthly basis based on the engineer's cost and the profit margin you aim to achieve.

So, even though your public-facing marketing collateral shows that your business is providing cloud-based services—setting up, maintaining, and troubleshooting the cloud—really, behind the scenes, the business is centered on acquiring talent—cloud setup and support talent. The product is not so much the cloud service that the customer side is seeing; rather, the product is *people* with cloud skills and competencies who will build and sell your cloud-building practice. Your product, underneath it all, is actually your engineer.

If you fail to build talent—in the example above, failing to bring in the top cloud engineer—then you will not have a quality service to offer. It is equally important that you be able to retain the talent you recruit. Continuing with our example, if you lose your cloud engineer, it means that the quality of your service might decline, and that can cascade into losing customers. Even if you manage to retain your customers after such a loss, the financial and time costs of finding, hiring, onboarding, and training a new cloud engineer, or any skilled employee, can be significant—employee churn has both hard and soft costs. If you don't maintain the quality of your talent, you cannot maintain the quality of your service and customer experience. Of course, every business will have processes in place to mitigate or minimize dips in their customer experience, but no matter what you do, the human being behind that process is the deciding factor when it comes to customer experience.

Delivering an exceptional customer experience is essential to commanding premium prices for your products and services. The customer experience is crucial for creating a referral-worthy product. The ability to provide top-notch service to both new and existing customers significantly influences your growth and profitability. High attrition of talent can reduce your profit margin and squeeze your EBITDA (Earnings Before Interest, Taxes, Depreciation, and Amortization).

Several talent-related factors can impact your EBITDA. Failing to establish a compassionate and stimulating culture, not implementing effective talent strategies, or lacking employee referrals can significantly increase your cost per hire. That means the cost of attrition becomes quite high when combined with talent marketing and other necessary strategies to fill positions. In the competitive "war for talent," the scarcity of skilled individuals further exacerbates the challenge of finding suitable candidates.

Protecting Your Brand

Your brand name is another crucial element tied to your ability to recruit and retain talent. If your customers' experience is less than exceptional or you cannot keep the promises you made to them, you can end up damaging your brand in the market. A lack of top talent can have a real negative impact: customer referrals will drop, your ability to deliver to existing customers will decline, and you will start to lose customers. High customer attrition and customer management costs will, in turn, affect your "churn," meaning the amount of revenue you generate from new customers. If you have a high churn rate, it will limit your growth and your profitability. One element impacts the next, and before you know it, your business is struggling to stay afloat or will fail altogether.

On the other hand, the reverse is also true. By successfully recruiting and retaining top talent, you increase the likelihood of attracting and retaining more customers, ensuring excellent customer experiences, and generating more customer referrals. This positive cascade enables you to build and protect your brand while simultaneously boosting profits and fostering growth.

Think of employer brand from the perspective of attracting talent—there is a correlation between attracting top talent and attracting top customers. Top talent wants to work for a caring brand, and top customers want to work with top talent in your company. If you can build your brand to attract top talent, attracting top customers will be a by-product. Top talent means top customers paying top dollar.

Professional Pain Points

Perhaps you and your business are already feeling the pressure of the talent war. Have you had trouble finding the right talent to help grow your business? Or maybe you are finding it increasingly difficult to motivate the talent you do have to deliver results. There are many day-to-day problems and frustrations in overcoming talent challenges.

Economic pressures have led to widespread layoffs in many sectors. So, that would mean an increased pool of talented people seeking gainful employment. But even with a rise in layoffs and redundancies, there is a surprising gap in supply and demand when it comes to top talent. For instance, let's look at some of the fastest-growing technology sectors. There is a new wave in development around artificial intelligence. The highest-paying job in the Bay Area right now is for prompt engineers, namely, people who can write prompts for ChatGPT. Similarly, the demand for cybersecurity engineers is simply so high that there simply are no engineers available to hire. No matter how great your idea or business model is, there is no way to execute it without talent.

Notably, as economic pressures increase, cybersecurity attacks are likely to increase. That, in turn, means the need for cybersecurity engineers and thinkers increases, putting even greater strain on the supply of talent in the field. With inflation on the rise and economic volatility, hackers are likely to increase their attacks to make more money. In times of economic hardship, there is usually a spike in the use of ransomware and other scams.

This works in parallel with the adoption of technology by more businesses, which means more businesses can be targeted by hackers, and therefore, more "cyber-heroes" are required to counter these attacks. However, hiring a full-time cybersecurity information security officer (CISO) engineer is often financially impractical due to the scarcity of qualified candidates. Many small businesses are turning to virtual CISOs through managed service providers (MSPs) as a cost-effective solution. Ensuring top talent safeguards your company (and your customers) is vital in this critical domain, where talent scarcity can make or break SMBs.

The demand and supply issue makes it challenging to engage and retain hot skills like cybersecurity, often leading to "quiet quitting" or wage theft as professionals take on additional jobs or freelance work on the side. This problem is worsened by the rise of work-from-home and hybrid work models. Employees may hold on to their positions but fail to produce value, directing their time and talents elsewhere, often taking on second jobs. Addressing this issue promptly is essential to prevent further depletion of your company's resources.

Leadership and Cultivating Talent

Another challenge in the talent war is being able to cultivate, develop, engage, and lead people once they have been onboarded. Many CEOs and people in leadership positions in the SMB space come from specific backgrounds—operations, accounting, finance, and technology—and their business models and cultures reflect that. They tend to be more techno-centric in the way they operate. They have the vision and the hard skills to build processes and services, but they can sometimes lack the soft skills to motivate people who think differently. The people component can be a real challenge, but getting it right is crucial. Your company scale is always going to hit a ceiling if you cannot grow your leadership and talent pool.

Anthony Mongeluzo, the president of PCS, a New Jersey-based IT services and consulting firm, and Danny Brickman, their service manager, highlight that delegating tasks is the most effective way to achieve growth. Many tech entrepreneurs think they can handle everything themselves, but to be truly smart, you must realize that scaling your business becomes challenging if you don't delegate. While maintaining a small team of 10, 15, or 20 people may give you control, it limits your ability to expand. Delegation is the key to unlocking growth.

So, as a leader, how do you identify, find, and develop talent? How do you onboard them? How do you retain them for the long term? You need to be able to scale beyond yourself. Otherwise, when it comes to growth, your scale is the scale of the company, and your speed on the people side is the speed of the company. Don't be the bottleneck for your own business! It is not enough simply to know that work is happening and money is coming in. You need to be able to manage your frontline people. You need to know how to train them and how to treat them to create engagement. The one common thing that you see time and time again in high-growth, high-profit companies is that they are very people-centric, and they have people-centric leaders and CEOs—Talentpreneurs.

If you think about what needs to happen for you to feel happy with your future—two or five years from now—what does that look like? Now think about the strategies that you are using to execute your vision. Without a doubt, your people strategy is going to be the greatest determining factor when it comes to executing your vision. If you can get the people component right—and the sooner, the better—the sooner you will be able to achieve your personal and professional vision of success.

A big part of that vision for most people is freedom and a good work-life balance. Everyone dreams of being their own boss, but many of us don't realize just how much work and stress comes along with that. The long days, sleepless nights, constant notifications, endless meetings, putting out fires, and shouldering the burdens of your business. You might think, *It's just this quarter. I'm going to work so hard*

this quarter, fix all the problems, and then I'll be streamlined.
But that is a kind of wishful thinking. That quarter will
become the next quarter, and before you know it, years have
passed this way. Your growth has stalled, and you're burnt
out. It is impossible to fix everything yourself.

If you don't want to be working 24/7, then you *must* find
people whom you can delegate to. You need people you can
trust. You need to find team members with complementary
skills and unique strengths. You need a team behind you
that you can delegate to with clear outcomes and then let
them fly. If your employees are happy, they are less likely
to go to your competition.

My friend and peer, Kelly Knight, has a 3-Point Formula
for attracting and retaining the best talent:

1. Invest in paying market rate compensation at the
   50th percentile across the organization; 75th percentile for key, stellar contributors.

2. Treat your people with genuine care and concern,
   and appreciate and value their contributions and
   God-given unique ability.

3. Empower team members, giving them the autonomy to collaborate, innovate and communicate with
   others to meet your company goals.

Turning the Tide Toward Talent

Every company will have its share of problems, some of
which we have outlined here. What most people do not
realize is that the most significant solution will come from
getting your people strategy right. You need the top talent
on your side (not the competition's!). Winning the talent

war means your company will become like a machine that grows by itself, like a gyroscope set in motion that keeps on spinning. As the saying goes, you want to reach the point where you have the time to work *on* the business, not work *in* the business.

Having the right talent to handle your day-to-day operations and execute your vision will grant you the freedom you've always desired as a business owner. You will finally have time to take your kids to sports activities, vacation with your family (without checking your emails!), travel the world, create new visionary products and services, explore emerging markets, and dream up new areas of expansion. The possibilities are endless. When you have less on your own plate, you will have greater bandwidth for everything else. Solving the talent war means that by being a great Talentpreneur, you can finally achieve your vision as an entrepreneur and create balance in your life.

Winning the talent war goes beyond just improving your business; it's a transformative step toward shaping your entire life positively. By having the right people on your team, you'll reclaim balance in your personal life, too—no more missing date nights or Little League games. You'll have the opportunity to craft the life you truly desire, and it all begins with nailing this crucial aspect. When you can attract, retain, and align top talent to deliver value to your customers, you'll find that everything else in your business falls perfectly into place. **Embrace this challenge and watch as it brings about a brighter and more fulfilling future.**

So, what can you do to become a great Talentpreneur and win the talent war? You must have a well-defined talent strategy. You need to have a world-class talent operating system, and that is just what I am going to share in this book.

In the coming chapters, we will explore talent success strategies using a world-class talent operating system. This book will show you how to build a happy and healthy community at work through Talentpreneurship.

2

My American Dream – Taxi to Talentpreneurship

From Pumping Gas to Serving MSPs

For the past twenty years, I have run a company that helps IT companies serve the SMB market. Our customers are IT-managed service providers, or MSPs, who serve SMBs. We provide technology solutions such as Network Operations Center (NOC), MSP-ready tech talent staffing, and talent management platforms to our customers. We have also built a technology business owners and leaders community called Build IT for leadership and entrepreneurial education. We are the undisputed talent authority in the MSP space. In this chapter, I will share with you how our company grew using a Talentpreneurship mindset, how we developed our expertise in talent management, and how knowledge will benefit your SMB, no matter what field you are in. But my own story starts somewhere else.

From Farmlands to Foreign Lands

I grew up on a farm in a village in India in the 1970s. India was different back then. It was before India entered the global economy as a major player. Back before the IT boom—even before home computers! Resources were limited. There was little infrastructure, particularly in rural areas.

I started learning English in the sixth grade while attending a local language school in my village, and that is where my journey began. English was a ticket to something beyond the edges of village life. When I graduated from high school, there were few local opportunities. The 1980s in India are sometimes referred to as a "lost decade." Rather than focusing on economic reform, then-Prime Minister Indira Gandhi was set on nationalizing the banks, which led to economic stagnation in the 90s even as the country modernized.[4] There was a lot of communal violence, terrorism, and security-related challenges in states such as Punjab. My life was at risk due to political upheaval and terrorism, so I had to leave—not just my village but India itself.

I moved to the New York City metro area in the United States—to Jersey City, New Jersey, to be exact—in 1993. The first time I saw the New York City skyline, as a kid from India who grew up without electricity, I was awestruck. I thought, *Am I still on planet Earth?* At night back home, the village was pitch black. New York City was like seeing the Milky Way rising from the Hudson River. The contrast between my humble beginnings and the dazzling cityscape before me was profound, and at that moment, I knew I had embarked on a life-changing journey.

I started living in an apartment with people my family knew from nearby villages back home in India. They were gas station attendants or cab drivers for New York City Yellow Cab. I only had $20 in my pocket and over $25,000 (USD) debt that my father had borrowed to help me get to the US. So, I needed to start earning money to pay back that debt and afford my living expenses. On top of that, the apartment I first moved into was very small. My roommates suggested that once I found a job, I should look for another place to stay. I did not have a driver's license, so I settled for the only odd job I could get.

I found a job pumping gas for five dollars an hour in Union, New Jersey, on Route 22. (New Jersey is perhaps the last remaining state where attendants pump your gas for you, even to this day.) I did not have the money yet for rent, let alone a deposit, so I moved into a storage room at the back of the garage. I remember that time so clearly because it was October. And it was cold. It was perhaps the first time that I experienced a cold. Where I'm from in the North of India, you never get snow; it is warm all year round. It was a shock to my system to have to be outside at all hours. I was working twelve-hour night shifts from 5:00 p.m. to 5:00 a.m. My hands were freezing. I was freezing. It felt like an overwhelming change, not just because of the temperature but because of everything it symbolized. Back in my hometown, we had always hired labor to handle the farm work, and now, here I was, pumping gas. It was a blow to my pride, a reminder of the stark contrast between my past and present reality.

Nevertheless, living in America was like a dream for me. In my first week, my roommates took me to Liberty Park in Jersey City to see the Statue of Liberty – because I did not have money to buy my own ferry and landmark visitor ticket. I remember thinking, *Wow, thank you, God; thank you, Waheguru. Look how blessed I am. That out of billions of people, I am so lucky that I get to come so close to this wonder of the world.* I was one of the billions who came to America for a better life, and just being in America was a big blessing.

I did find a new apartment not long after I started at the gas station. I remember, in my search, mentioning to my friends how nice it would be to find an apartment with hot water, as theirs had. It had been so luxurious taking hot showers—a new experience for a village boy! I had only ever "showered" using the old-style manual pump from the well on our farm, which of course, drew the water up cold, straight from the ground. My friends laughed and told me, "Sunny, you will have a hard time finding an apartment here that *doesn't* have hot water!" What passed for luxury in India was just the norm in America.

After about a year of working at the gas station, I knew I had to do something else. I asked my roommates, "Hey, guys, what is next?" They told me I could make a lot more money driving cabs in New York. So, I went to Queens, NY, took a two-week course, memorized every street and alley in the five boroughs (no GPS back then!), and got my Taxi and Limousine Commission for New York City. I went from being a new immigrant who had never even driven a car before to taking passengers here, there, and everywhere. It was a big challenge for a village boy—not to mention the added challenge of learning a different kind of English on the streets of New York.

The pay was better, but driving a cab in New York in the early '90s had challenges of its own. It was not the safest place to be at that time (luckily, still safer than Punjab!). Mayor Rudolph Giuliani was just starting his "tough on crime" platform, and his priority was "civic cleanup" of Times

Square and the Meatpacking District. I was still working the night shift, 5:00 p.m. to 5:00 a.m., and getting robbed was a real risk. This was in the days before credit cards and electronic payments became the norm. Everything was done with cash. And I was still living in Jersey City, which meant I had to take the PATH train to the city, and you could also easily be robbed on the subway.

It wasn't unusual for passengers to run off without paying their fares; that was perhaps the best-case scenario. Worse, sometimes they would not pay and steal all your cash or beat you up. There was no partition between the driver and the rest of the cab, so safety was a constant issue. Once, in Harlem, someone threw a brick through the windshield of the cab—this was after I'd just been robbed. You get the picture.

Even so, I enjoyed that experience because I learned so much. To this day, you can tell me an address anywhere in the city, and I know exactly where it is (other than famous '90s restaurants and bars that no longer exist) and how to get there. It is a great party trick to drive in New York without needing a GPS. More than that, your life experience will always help you somewhere down the line.

The Keys to the College

Part of the reason I was working so hard, why I pressed on despite the robberies and risks, was to repay my father's debt. He had used our farmland as collateral to send me to the US. From my first day, my main goal was to pay back that money to my father so that he could be debt free once more. Between pumping gas in Union and driving cabs in New York, I had saved enough to pay him back within about three years. The day I paid him back, it felt like a humongous weight was lifted.

With my debt paid to my father, I started thinking about what I wanted to do next. I was earning about $4,000 a month at that time. I always had an entrepreneurial side, and I considered doing what so many of my friends were doing: saving up to buy my own gas station. I figured that if I was making about $48,000 a year, I could save money over the next two or three years. With a $100,000 deposit, I might buy a gas station. They are easy to run and pull in a consistent, reliable business for uneducated immigrants. That is why many of the gas stations in New Jersey are owned by Punjabis.

My roommates and friends encouraged me to follow that same path. If I took the college route, which I was thinking about, they thought I would not make any money, and even if I did, it would be eaten up in taxes. But I was committed to my education. I figured if I went to college, I could take my family one generation ahead of everyone else. Rather than planning to one day send my kids to college and live vicariously through their experience, I'm going to do it myself. And if I do, I will be able to guide them.

I was driven by the idea of lifelong learning, and I believed firmly in having the courage to give up on short-term gains in favor of the long-term. Even then, I was thinking strategically. I wanted to forge and follow my own unique path.

I called my father. I told him I wanted to pursue a college degree. I wanted to do everything I could for my family, so I asked if he needed me to keep working and keep sending money or if I could begin college.

He said, "You know, if you are really serious about completing college, then go."

I knew what I wanted to do, but I had no idea how to go about it. Neither did any of my roommates. It was totally new territory. I didn't even know which colleges were nearby. Remember, we did not have Google or smartphones to look up information. But every now and then, Lady Luck smiles at us all. One day, as I was walking to the train station from my apartment, heading into the city to pick up my cab for the night, I noticed a billboard for Hudson County Community College (HCCC).

I knew that if I wanted to go to college, I needed to do the groundwork myself. However, I didn't even know what I might need in order to get accepted. The next day, I woke up early, stopped by the college, and picked up a course catalog. But even that was a challenge. I had a hard time explaining what I wanted because, in India, a course catalog is called a prospect. I asked the admission office for one, and they were stone-faced. "What is a prospect?" they asked. But after much effort and communication via body language, I managed to convey what I wanted, and I came away with the catalog in hand. A small victory and the first step towards my college education.

On the train to work that evening, I flipped through the pages of the catalog. I noticed a picture of a man wearing a turban, and below the image, it read, "Dr. J.S. Duggal, Assistant Dean, Science and Technology, Hudson County Community College." I recognized his last name straight away as it was a common name in Punjab. *Great,* I thought. *This man can guide me in the right direction because he can speak my language.* I did not waste any time.

The next day I started exploring the idea of meeting him. I found his office and spoke to his secretary about setting up a meeting. Now, secretaries are gatekeepers for their employers. Madeline, Dr. Duggal's secretary, was no different. She wanted to know the purpose of the visit, given that I was not even yet a student at HCCC. And for my part, the idea of booking an appointment with someone was new to me. It took a couple of visits, but eventually, I convinced Madeline that Dr. Duggal was my uncle and that I needed his help. She relented and made the appointment for me.

In our meeting, I explained everything to Dr. Duggal, my whole life story and all my hopes and dreams: that I came here on my own, that I had been working as a cab driver but wanted more, that I wanted to earn my bachelor's degree, attend medical school, and return to India to work as a doctor.

Dr. Duggal pointed out all the hurdles I would face. I did not have a green card at that time, which he explained meant that I would not be eligible for student loans or financial aid. I was still driving a taxi but having just paid off my debt to my father; I had no savings. How could I afford to pay for college without savings, financial support, and a green card?

"If you are planning to pay for medical college by driving a cab, it is going to be extremely difficult. Almost impossible. But how do you feel about working with computers?" Dr. Duggal said. This was the tail end of 1995. The internet was starting to find its way into people's homes. Windows 95 had become the biggest online service in the world virtually overnight. Computers were the next big thing. He said, "In India, normally, people excel in math and science. I understand you want to be a doctor, but what do you think about this instead?"

I thought it was a great idea. If there were big opportunities in computers, I wanted to explore that. He advised me to take an English as a Second Language (ESL) or basic English class to improve my language skills and help me with the English assessment test required for college enrollment. And that is where I started at Hudson County

Community College in January 1996. I was taking about eighteen credits, mostly 101 and intro classes to begin with, and continued driving a taxi at night. As a non-resident student, my college fees were twice as high, and I had to pay cash in full.

I completed two years at Hudson County Community College and then was able to transfer to the New Jersey Institute of Technology (NJIT) for computer engineering. In the last two years of college, I began tutoring on the side and building computers for people in my community and my temple. This is where my interest in building and fixing computers started to blossom. I would go to computer shows and buy all the components—motherboards, hard drives, memory—and put it all together. I would make a small markup, but it was still more cost-effective for buyers than what the big box stores were charging them. I fancied myself a bit like Michael Dell, building white boxes in his garage. It felt good, too, to have a presence in my community. I was the only college-educated person at that time, and people often came to me for advice. I was happy to be building my reputation and helping people at the same time. I completed my bachelor's degree in 2000.

From Taxi to Tech

I graduated in 2000, and then in 2001, the economy crashed. It was not a great time to be a recent grad and a new job seeker. My English, while much improved, was still something of an impediment in interviews, so I had a hard time finding a job. Eventually, I landed a position at a public relations firm in New York City as a systems administrator. It was a small business with a small budget. The average salary for a systems administrator at that time in New York was around $60,000. When the owner of the firm, Morris Silver, offered me the job, he said, "I don't want to offend you because you are a computer engineer. You have the degree. You have the qualifications, but I can only offer you $29,000. This is the only budget I have."

I was overjoyed. I could have cared less about the money at that point. All I wanted was to get out of driving cabs and get into tech, doing the work I loved and that I had worked so hard to learn. I was not going to pass up this opportunity. I said, "Morris, you decide what you want to pay me. Just tell me when I can come to work."

I was determined to prove myself. I was just so hungry to join the professional sector after college. I did not want to be a failure, especially after all that hard work and all the money I had spent.

The office was situated in the heart of midtown Manhattan, precisely on 47th Street and 3rd Avenue, occupying the 23rd floor. It was a dramatic shift from my previous job, where I had worked grueling twelve-hour night shifts, seven days a week, for a staggering four or five years. Now, I had transitioned to a regular nine-to-five, Monday-to-Friday schedule. But strangely, it felt like part-time work, leaving me with a sense of dissatisfaction. I yearned for a feeling of true accomplishment.

Although I was grateful for the opportunity to get my foot in the door, surviving on a salary of $29,000 in New York City was a financial stretch. To add to the pressure, I had recently tied the knot, and we had to find a place of our own. My wife had moved from Canada to be with me and was pursuing her master's degree on a student visa, which meant she couldn't work. With increasing responsibilities and expenses, I felt the weight of these new challenges bearing down on me.

I still had my TLC license to drive taxis. The TLC license was like the small-time entrepreneur's golden ticket in New York before Uber was a thing. You can show up at any garage at 5:00 pm, show them your license, pay your $100 to rent a cab for the night, and make your money. It is an excellent safety net. A great trade to fall back on. Which is exactly what I did. I did not feel I was doing enough working nine to five, so I set up an arrangement with a friend. He rented a cab during the daytime and dropped it off for me to drive from 5:00 p.m. to midnight.

I maintained that demanding schedule for a year, burning the candle at both ends. In 2001, my wife and I had our first child. By that time, I had developed many new tech-based skills, becoming proficient in fixing servers, firewalls, and routers. As I looked at my growing expertise, a powerful idea started to take shape in my mind: Instead of spending nights driving taxis, I could leverage my skills to offer IT support to other businesses as a subcontractor. That is where IT By Design was born.

I always wanted to do more, be helpful and useful, earn more, and make more of myself. People in business often talk about "elevator pitches," a quickfire description of an idea, product, or company that you can pitch to someone in the time it takes to ride an elevator. Now, most people don't mean this in the literal sense. But I used to meet people in the elevator all the time. The PR firm was on the 23rd floor. I would chat with people and make small talk every day. "Who do you work for? What floor are you on?" That sort of thing.

There were all sorts of businesses in my building: law firms, staffing and marketing firms, and small companies. One day I thought, with all these other businesses, there must be a need for IT services. I spoke with my boss, Morris, to ensure there was no conflict of interest. He said that if it was outside of normal business hours and I was not serving any other PR firms (i.e., the competition), he saw no reason I should not go for it. He was a very fair-minded person.

I went home and created a brochure for "Kaila Consulting: IT services at a cost-effective rate." I added my cell phone number and a few other details. I printed a few copies every week. And every day during my lunch hour, I would visit every floor of the building and leave a Kaila Consulting brochure with the receptionist. Every floor. Every office. It might have been a long shot, but my advantage was that not only was I offering services outside of normal hours—evenings and weekends when no one else wanted to be working—I was only charging twenty-five dollars an hour. It was a steal compared to the going rate for IT consultants at the time, which averaged around $150 an hour.

Soon after starting my IT venture, an unexpected call came from a law firm upstairs. The voice on the other end pleaded, "My computer has a virus. Can you help me?" It was a defining moment—I had landed my very first customer! As fate would have it, when an employee from the same law firm moved to another firm, they reached out to me again. "Sunny, the computers here are a mess. Can you come and fix them?" Without hesitation, I took on the challenge, and just like that, I had my second customer. The business grew on a referral basis. My first three or four customers all came from the office building on 47th Street.

By 2003, I was ready to step out on my own. I changed the name of the business from Kaila Consulting to IT By Design, which remains the name today. Once more, I approached Morris and said, "I need to start my own business. I'm getting established, and I can earn more on my own."

But I had proved myself above and beyond to Morris. He was not about to let me go. "Sunny," he said, "you can do this here. You can do this for me." He offered to raise my salary to $60,000. I would be doubling my salary within two years of starting. I could not turn him down. I worked for him during the week at the office, and then I would drive to his home in Queens on the weekends to be his on-call IT concierge. It was hard work, but with that, I was able to generate more surplus income, making it possible to hire another tech for my company.

The business was booming. I had another offer from a company called Atrium Staffing. They offered me $120,000 a year, but they wanted me full-time as a consultant, which later, just like Morris, became our managed services customer. I could not believe their offer. It seemed like yesterday that I was making five dollars an hour at the gas station in Union. I would be lying if I said I did not battle with a degree of imposter syndrome. I did not yet have confidence in myself. I doubted I was worth that, but only a fool would turn them down. That is when my wife joined our business, and we hired a second tech. I continued to perform customers' tech work after business hours and on weekends. We continued to build our customer list, which really seemed to build itself. Our service was exceptional, and our name spread quickly by word of mouth.

Find What Makes You Unique and Build on It

I had grown accustomed to often being the only Indian guy at MSP tech conferences, which was still a space dominated by Caucasian Americans. Some people might see that as a disadvantage, but my view was that Waheguru (God) had given me something unique. All the big tech companies—Microsoft, Apple, Dell—were setting up 24/7 delivery centers in India for their tech support. I knew this was someplace I would have an edge. Our customers in the city were asking for true 24/7 service. Here in the States, it was hard to find people who wanted to work nights and weekends.

In 2008, I traveled to India to conduct a feasibility study. I ended up hiring five techs, Dell engineers, and they became our full-time engineers. I built 24/7 delivery capability by using my India office for my own managed services customers in New York City.

I was part of a few professional groups—peer groups made up of people, usually CEOs, who have similar businesses but in different cities or not in direct competition. It is a great tool for learning from each other's experiences, from failures and successes alike. Well, my peers started to take notice. They saw that my business was growing much faster than theirs, and they wanted to know the secret of my success. "What the heck are you doing that we are not doing?" they asked.

So I started helping them, just as friends. I would lend them the services of my tech team in India. But it got to the point where I was doing them favors all the time. I could not continue to donate services for free. But that gave me a new idea for how to expand my business. I could build a new product to serve my competitors if that was where the demand was. So, around 2014 or 2015, I stopped selling to direct customers and started selling to Managed Service Providers (MSPs), to my competitors, and to companies just like IT By Design. Our target customer changed, and our growth accelerated. IT companies throughout the US started to use our services because we were available any day, any time, thanks to backend remote capability. We were not geographically limited to Manhattan-area tech businesses.

Today, IT By Design employs six hundred employees. We are one of the top 10 biggest privately held MSPs in America. We sell our services to over four hundred IT-based MSPs, companies similar to how IT by Design started. I like to credit New York City as part of my success. Having cut our teeth on the mean streets of the Big Apple, we were sure to be able to deliver anywhere. The toughest customer in the world is a New York customer. So, as Sinatra famously sang, if you can make it there, you can make it anywhere.

Even better, our growth was organic. I mentioned in the first chapter how an MSB's product is their talent, their people. IT By Design grew organically—not through mergers and acquisitions. We haven't acquired any other companies. We grew by hiring more and more talent— through Talentpreneurship. And it was important that, as we did that, we maintained the high standard with which we began. I made sure that we were always meeting the US standards for talent quality in hiring, training, and contin-uous development. It set us apart from other organizations with similar global capacities, but which left customers and customers with bad experiences and poor results (remember Zenith?).

It is a lot of work to maintain that high standard. Do you know how many interviews you have to conduct to recruit, maintain and grow to a team of six hundred people? It goes without saying that I have had plenty of hands-on experience attracting, hiring, developing, and retaining the right talent. Moreover, I have experience in successfully building and managing remote teams, even before COVID, with very diverse talent from different cultures.

Lady Liberty and the American Dream

It is perhaps not in vogue anymore to talk about the American Dream, but before we move on to the nitty gritty of winning the Talent Wars, let me leave you with this deeply personal story. I came to the US in 1993 as a village boy who arrived with nothing but debt of about $25,000 to my father, who had borrowed the money to send me here. One of my first sights in America was the Statue of Liberty, which my friends took me to see during my first week living in New Jersey.

Things came full circle for me in 2021 when I rented out the entirety of Liberty Island for one component of a three-day conference we were hosting for our customers. As I was standing there on that day, I was so emotional. Remember that at one point in my life, I did not have the money to buy a visitor ticket, let alone rent the entire island. The sense of freedom I felt at that moment overwhelmed me and moved me to tears. I reflected on the freedoms that America gives you—no matter who you are or where you come from. You have that equal opportunity. The American Dream. It felt like just the other day I was standing in New Jersey, looking at the Statue from far away, with nothing more to my name than hope and a hunger to succeed. And even then, it felt like a blessing. I never in my life dreamed that I would one day be able to rent out that entire island.

I looked out over the crowds, customers of a business I built from the ground up. My wife and I were standing under an American flag. To the right, I saw all of our guests enjoying the party under the gaze of the Statue of Liberty. To the left was the Freedom Tower. It was an incredible moment. A truly American moment. People say the American dream is dead, but it is not: you must work hard for it. I am here to tell you that the American dream is alive. Success is just around the corner. But I could not have achieved this dream without my amazing wife and the incredible talent I had around me.

In this chapter, I wanted to share what helped me achieve my American dream. My key lessons are: Dream big, be a lifelong learner, work hard and smart, have grit, know yourself and your life purpose, and finally, surround yourself with great people who have a well-defined, shared sense of purpose to build a healthy community at work. My father's advice, "Surround yourself with great people, add value to them, and success will follow you," was my primary guide for building a community of great human beings at work and in my personal life. It is all about relationships, teamwork, and collaboration with the right people.

Regardless of the field you are in, my father's advice and the lessons I've learned can be applied to benefit your SMB.

3

Staffing Up in a Post-Pandemic World

The COVID-19 pandemic increased the trend toward employee entitlement, which began in the 1990s with the widespread adoption of technology. I define "employee entitlement" as a sense that many team members today possess that their needs are paramount and the needs of the employer are secondary. The last twenty years have seen a sea change in terms of office environments, employers' roles, and employee expectations. It used to be hard to find a job after college. People were limited by what work was available in their geographic area. They were drawn to work at whatever factory served the major industry or whatever companies had offices in their town or city, and they held onto those jobs for longer. There was a loyalty shared between employer and employee. Continuity was part and parcel of building a career and a business.

Now, with advances in technology and infrastructure, many employees and job seekers can essentially work from anywhere in the world. And with that, the mindset has largely shifted to, "I can find a job easily, and I will do what I want." This, in turn, led to a growing shift in the balance of control, moving away from the employer and into the hands of the employee. The pandemic sped this up even more, adding further pressure to small and mid-sized businesses.

Now you can hire workers from all over the world, which means that employers are often struggling to find talent within their borders. Even if you can find the right talent, the employee mindset has shifted, making it harder to retain top talent. With Talent Wars in full swing, companies are struggling to find and retain good people. All this adds to your already rising costs as a company.

What's missing from today's post-pandemic landscape is an integrated talent system built for today's challenges that provides a framework to effectively manage talent strategy. So what can you do?

In the Room vs. On Zoom

So, what are the challenges for staffing in a post-pandemic world? What makes it harder now than in the past? When it comes to the staffing life cycle—hiring, developing, and retaining people—everything has changed. For example, it used to be common practice for job seekers to go to job fairs. These were open house events where potential candidates could connect with companies, network, and perhaps get an invitation to come into the office to interview at a later date. Candidates could then do a meet and greet session in a group, see the facility, and gather more information about the job and work environment—and it also gave employers a better view of their candidates.

It was a more relaxed atmosphere, and sessions tended to be longer than just an interview—certainly longer than most interviews done via video call—so there was ample time for both parties to talk. Candidates learned about the company and potential job opportunities, and employers learned more about individual candidates and how they might contribute to the company. Relationship building was part of the process from the outset.

In contrast, almost everything to do with the hiring process in the post-pandemic world has shifted to virtual. Many job seekers do not want the hassle of having to travel in for an interview. It takes time and costs money on fuel or other transport—all for a thirty-minute or hour-long interview that might not lead to anything. So instead, many interviews at least begin remotely, though they may move to in-person interviews in the later stages. And indeed, it is not unusual for interviews to be conducted wholly online. That means that right away, before you have even hired someone, there is already a real distance established between you and your talent.

Changes have also been made to the way training and onboarding are done. Training used to be conducted in person, but now, because a lot of companies are hiring without geographic restrictions, this is done virtually, as well. Or, in the instances where companies do still hire locally, many businesses and their employees have kept the hybrid models introduced in the post-quarantine days of the pandemic. You might not meet the people you work with every day in person for months—if ever.

So, what effect, if any, does this have on teamwork, collaboration, and productivity? Previously, collaboration used to be in person. Maybe your team worked in a sales pod, and there was a lot of in-person collaboration in the bullpen. Maybe you had an engineering or tech team collaborating on problem-solving or doing technical work to complete projects. There used to be a lot of knowledge sharing in one area—physically, in one room. Now because people are not sitting right next to each other, the collaboration is very different. Of course, there are tools like Microsoft Teams and Zoom available to help connect your people to each other, but there is no substitute for getting people in the same room.

When two engineers are sitting right next to each other, picking each other's brains, learning from each other's experiences, and solving that ticket together, they are going to be better equipped to tackle a network issue, technical problem, or project implementation challenges. And it is very hard to replicate that virtually. That is where the biggest challenge lies—in particular for tech companies: how do you best position an experienced technical lead or level-three engineer so that they can help a level one or level two engineer when they are both working remotely? You could be losing out on valuable insights and problem-solving for your company's challenges by not having people collaborating effectively with one another.

As for productivity, when someone is physically sitting in the office, there are certain expectations. Psychologically it is very different sitting in your home office or on your couch. In the office, you are part of the team. And with that comes an awareness that you can be seen by your teammates and managers. If there are less disciplined employees in your company, an office environment is more conducive to reducing distractions and providing them with support to help them focus. That boosts productivity, and productivity is part and parcel of profitability.

Under a work-from-home or hybrid work scheme, it is important for employers to understand that there are bound to be people on their team who may not be self-disciplined. Of course, every team will have a mix of people and personalities. Some will be able to self-manage their workload, minimize distractions, and generally be self-disciplined. But let's face it, even the most dedicated worker is likely to have more distractions at home than in an office, especially when some people may not have a designated workspace or home office. And whether it is scrolling their newsfeed or social media, letting the dog out, making another pot of coffee, or making a snack for their kids—there is no end to what can distract you at home. If employees cannot self-manage, they might easily lose an hour of work time in this way. Inevitably, that means they are not contributing as much as they should to your company.

On the flip side, there are also employees who are more productive at home. Without the distractions of colleagues and coworkers, some people have found they can focus more on work at home than in the office. Working from home also saves people time, energy, and money traveling in and out of the office. Some people might feel less drained if they can avoid spending hours a day commuting and instead can simply walk downstairs and begin their workday. They might feel less stressed and, therefore, more focused. Who among us has not felt our blood pressure rise when being cut off in traffic on our way to that big meeting?

So productivity is a big issue in the post-COVID work world. There are generally two categories of workers and worker output: either productivity levels are very low because employees are not able to make the transition and self-manage at home, or on the other hand, some people are really doing their part very well. Your job as an employer or manager is to know how best to support your employees—whichever category they fall into—so that they can best serve your customers.

One of the other big obstacles to people working from home, especially if your employees or business are customer-facing, is infrastructure. When your people work from home, you are relying on their home infrastructure—and these are not going to be enterprise-level networks. If their home Wi-Fi goes down and an important call drops, or even if it is simply a poor voice quality call, that will impact the customer experience. There are only so many controls you can put in place to ensure the reliability of the network because everyone is using their home network. It can be really difficult under these circumstances to deliver the same world-class experience that you are able to deliver from an office with an enterprise-level internet connection (and a backup line if that one line goes down).

It is crucial to recognize the significance of this issue, especially in light of the current trend where companies are employing a global workforce. Many tech companies are now looking to emerging markets such as India, the Philippines, and Vietnam to bolster their workforce with international talent. This is a favorable choice for numerous SMBs. However, one must consider that people working from home in these countries may face a higher likelihood of encountering network problems, whether caused by electrical or internet infrastructure issues or natural disasters and environmental factors. These challenges can have a direct impact on both customer experience and employee productivity.

This is all to say that who your talent is and where they are have a palpable, direct impact on everything from customer experience to profitability. It is a key piece of the puzzle when it comes to running a successful business and winning the Talent Wars.

Do Your People Measure Up?

As we can see, when your people are working from home, one of the biggest challenges is measuring their productivity and engagement. How do you know they are not just raiding the fridge or scrolling Instagram or watching TikTok videos? How do you know they are actually working?

There are a number of systems available to help employers measure and manage productivity. If there is any misalignment of expectations or performance between a manager and an employee, then it is important to put those measures in place. For example, if an employee thinks they are overproducing by saving on travel time, but the manager thinks that person is not meeting productivity expectations, then there are tools like goal setting, productivity alignment, and effective time utilization systems to help solve this problem. The employee enters their hours worked and a brief summary of what they have done. Then, the manager can review that timesheet on a weekly basis in order to gain a fuller understanding of how that person is truly utilizing their time at work.

The Entitlement Mindset

The shift to this virtual model in the last two or three years, combined with the fact that talent does not need to be geographically tied to their workplace, means that there are significantly more opportunities available than there is talent to fill them. That has led to a shift in the balance of power from employers to employees. You see it in every company. People are less likely to stay in a job if there is any kind of friction. The notion of grit, of having to prove yourself and your value, is starting to fall by the wayside. The number of employees who are willing to go above and beyond, who are motivated and engaged, is dwindling. Spending your whole career at one company is a thing of the past. Employees know that if they leave a job today, they can have five or ten opportunities elsewhere the minute they walk out of the virtual door.

In the post-COVID world, there has been a general shift in mindset and work ethic. The days of an employee doing whatever it took to keep his or her job, of really pushing themselves, those days are gone. They are quick to throw up their hands and quick to quit. Sites like LinkedIn and Indeed have become like Tinder for job seekers. It is all too easy to swipe right on your next potential employer and ghost your current one. People do not fight for their relationships anymore, including the employer-employee relationship. It is too easy to simply move on to the next thing—and the next thing, and the next thing after that.

Employees think that, as an employer, you need them more than they need you. (And they are right.) That means that you need to think about your talent strategy very differently today than you did yesterday. The way you think about building your company culture also needs to shift. Otherwise, there are a whole host of knock-on effects that will negatively impact your business.

The entitlement mindset among employees can lead to higher attrition rates for employers. In the tech industry, where engineers often interact directly with customers, this can have a significant impact on customer relationships. If your company is constantly losing employees and undergoing changes due to a sense of entitlement among the workforce, it will negatively affect the customer experience. Finding replacements takes time, and with each staff change, the hiring, training, and onboarding process restarts, which can be especially challenging for small to mid-sized businesses.

There is generally not a great deal of surplus engineering labor capacity; thus, when someone leaves, the company cannot serve the same customer the same way. Processes should be strong to avoid building a person-based experience; nonetheless, attrition does impact customer experience. And how does it look to the customer if you have to repeatedly introduce them to new staff, starting the relationship over from scratch again and again? What is really at stake with high attrition is the customer experience.

The new entitlement mindset can also affect your ability to manage talent effectively. There is an awareness among managers that if they push an employee just a little bit too much, there is a higher probability that they will leave. If you drive accountability, the result might not be improved performance; instead, the only result could be more friction. If that is the case, how are you supposed to encourage and motivate talent to work harder for you?

Where in the World Are Your People?

The developments in technology and the cultural shift towards remote work and hybrid models have, as we have discussed, tipped the balance of control toward employees. But, in some ways, it is a two-way street. While employees can now easily find employers anywhere in the world, employers in many industries, especially tech, also have a global pool of potential candidates to pick from.

A big issue for many SMBs is that limited technical talent is available in the US. The US is still the world leader when it comes to technology adoption, innovation, and everything else that goes along with the tech space. But in terms of the technical knowledge workers have versus the technical opportunities in the US, there is a huge skill set gap. Big companies tend to sweep up top talent before SMBs even have a chance. This is especially true for companies that deliver cybersecurity or cloud security and other critical services. There is not enough talent to meet the demand of the market.

When deciding whether to hire locally or internationally for your company, several factors come into play, especially considering the specific role you're looking to fill. Certain positions in cybersecurity, for example, may have compliance standards that necessitate hiring within the US. This requirement often arises due to the customers these employees will be serving.

On the other hand, some roles are better suited for talent abroad. Positions that require working during nighttime or weekends can be more easily filled by hiring internationally, as it might be challenging to find suitable candidates domestically. In many cases, individuals in the US prefer not to work during unsociable hours. However, depending on the location of your international hires, those evening hours may align perfectly with their regular working hours, making it a better fit for their schedule.

While there used to be some reservations about the quality available when hiring international talent, that, too, has changed. People are more open, and there is now widespread adoption of the practice across industries, especially in the tech sector. It no longer matters where your talent is located; it matters if they are performing and delivering on customer experience. Asia has come on the scene as a major player in the tech space. Over the last decade, the region has accounted for 52 percent of global growth in tech-company revenues, according to the McKinsey Global Institute.[5] The region has been steadily increasing its share of the global IT services market, which is expected to continue to grow by 5–6 percent per year over the next five years.[6] It is no wonder that US businesses are tapping into these international talent pools to help meet demand.

There are two main reasons for this change, in addition to the advances in technology and infrastructure that make it possible, to begin with. One is cost, and the other is the availability of good talent. So let's break those down.

The average rates of compensation for engineering talent are positively galloping in front of inflation. That can have a huge impact on your budget. We have seen salaries skyrocket significantly, especially in the last three years. In some cases, engineers were asking for double their salaries post-COVID as compared to pre-COVID. There was an unprecedented wave of pay increases in the tech space. For example, a cybersecurity engineer might have cost $50,000 per year in 2018 or 2019, and today that same engineer is likely to cost closer to $80,000 to $90,000 per year. *The Wall Street Journal* has noted, "Wage inflation in the technology sector is accelerating, pressuring companies to boost compensation for key roles by 20% or more as they compete for a limited pool of workers skilled in areas such as cloud computing and data science." They additionally note that high-demand jobs like cloud architects are on the higher end, with average increases of twenty-five percent and upwards.[7] Analysts expect the trend to continue, with the demand for pay increases rising even further in 2023.

Unfortunately, it is not always possible to pass those costs on to your customers. Instead, it eats into your profitability. Your profit margins shrink because customers will always resist price increases, and you need to increase your employees' salaries if you want to retain your top talent and keep them from walking.

So today, not only is talent hard to find and harder to manage, but talent also costs more. As an employer, executive, or manager, you want to deliver. You want to deliver on your brand promise to your customers. You want to deliver on the contract you signed. But what happens when the Talent Wars get in your way? That is exactly what C-level executives have been struggling with the most in the last two or three years: to grow without compromising profitability. There is a lot of work; there is no shortage of projects and customers to be had, but growth without compromising profitability is a major challenge. With inflation rising globally, in some countries, as much as nine, ten, and eleven percent, many SMBs have no choice other than to raise prices for their customers. That can sometimes mean losing customers to your competitors if they can underprice you or if they are better able to maintain their talent.

Cost increases are especially hard on SMBs that have fixed-price contracts. If you have agreed to deliver services over a given period at a fixed rate, but your costs are starting to creep up with rising salaries and general inflation, it can be a real squeeze on your budget. Some companies get stuck in this cycle and are certainly losing money this way. They might hope to plant some seeds early on to recoup when the time renewal rolls around, and they can sign on for a new rate, but it is a bad position to be in.

Staffing Up for Success

So what do you do to staff up in the post-COVID, entitlement mindset era? It is important to lay the groundwork from the beginning. That starts with putting best practices in place during the hiring process and making sure the people you are hiring have everything they need to be successful and perform their best. Do they have a dedicated, noise-free, distraction-free space to work from home? Do they have the materials and infrastructure they need, like a quality desktop or laptop computer, proper desk and chair, and good home Wi-Fi? Make a checklist of everything they will need to do their job to the best of their ability and, if they are customer-facing, everything they need to give your customers the best possible experience, too.

During the interview process, make sure you test their home infrastructure space and check the quality. That should be non-negotiable. In the same way that great companies won't compromise on culture fit, you should not compromise on the basic needs and home workspace infrastructure for your team. If that means you have to wait an extra week or two to hire the right people or get them set up, then wait. It is so critical to have the right people and to make all those checks at the beginning of the relationship if you want to deliver a top-quality customer experience—and employee experience, as well. We will talk more about talent acquisition strategies in the talent operating system chapter.

Next, you want to have a solid engagement plan. In the post-COVID era, employers need to look at things very differently in terms of having programs to engage people. At my company, we call this our "Life By Design" plan. We want to take care of people in all aspects of their lives, not just their careers. In today's marketplace, it is all about deeply caring about your talent—and demonstrating this through programs that benefit your whole health and wellness. For example, my company offers employees the opportunity to work with life coaches for mental wellness programs on a weekly basis. We host yoga and meditation classes that employees can sign up for. We have even provided sleep doctors and experts to educate people on sleep-related health issues.

Our key focus is to support our people's overall well-being. To achieve this, we utilize our proprietary tool called "Team GPS" to measure and manage their engagement level. By using this technology, we can identify any early signs of disengagement, allowing us to address the issue before it escalates into a larger problem. Part of building a great company culture is including events and activities for your team that are not performance related. For example, my company hosts quarterly get-togethers and other fun events that staff can choose to participate in. These activities foster a sense of camaraderie among the team and management. By getting to know each other on a personal level and feeling supported in all areas of life, it strengthens loyalty among the team members.

There is one more piece of the puzzle when it comes to staffing up for success. It is equally important to make sure that people are growing within the company. We always try to promote from within wherever possible. It is all about culture and community.

Where Do We Go from Here?

Staffing up in a post-pandemic world is harder than ever, and if you are experiencing these issues, you are not alone. That is simply the state of the talent market. Even if you treat your people exceptionally well, and you have meaningful processes to engage with them and track that engagement, you are still likely to see ripples of the post-pandemic changes to your business—whether it is how you manage your talent, how and where your team works, or the costs and profitability of your company.

The goal is to be above the benchmark for your industry. At my company, one way we measure our success is in comparison to how much other companies had to raise their prices and how much attrition they had to deal with. We recorded best-in-class numbers, but even those best-in-class numbers, when you compare that with our past numbers, show that we, too, have felt the impact, albeit managed it well.

So in the next chapter, we will discuss how to determine what your business's needs really are. For example, do you need your people to be in the building, can they be remote, or would your business benefit from a mix of both? We will take a look at solutions to some of the problems we have discussed here—how to hire talent more effectively, whether you are hiring people in the wrong places if there are ways to better understand what your employees' needs are—so that you can avoid those problems and grow your business.

4

What Does Your Business Really Need?

I t may seem like the work-from-home world hit overnight, but it has been a long time in the making. Since the dawn of the internet and the ever-increasing portion of our lives and businesses moving online, in some ways, the modern workspace was inevitable; COVID-19 only accelerated the process. Today, we live in a post-pandemic world where some people insist on working remotely, some want a mix of working in the office and working at home, and some want to work solely at the office. How do you manage those conflicting desires while balancing the business's needs?

Take restaurants, for example. Working from home does not work for the customer-facing staff—waiters, bartenders, kitchen staff, hosts, and so on—but those on the corporate side could work from home. There are different needs for different roles. The same goes for the IT industry. Some team members can work from home, and some need to be out in the field, fixing things. With law or accounting, there's a balance between working from home and having customer meetings, which need to be in person. Same with telemedicine, which can replace some but not all patient visits.

In this chapter, we'll explore how to balance your needs as an employer with your team members' desires to work the way they want to work. What is the way forward for talent strategies, especially when what employees want may be different from what the company needs?

The future of the workplace is undoubtedly leaning towards a hybrid or fully remote model. This shift is particularly evident in professional services, such as IT companies, where much of the business is conducted online. While there may still be some companies that insist on an entirely onsite approach, this can pose a challenge in attracting top talent. Nowadays, skilled individuals prioritize flexibility in their work arrangements. Consequently, the workplace of the future will largely be divided into two main models: fully remote or hybrid. So, how do you determine what model is the right one for you?

The Goldilocks Model

We all know the story of Goldilocks and the three bears, and more importantly, the moral of the story: what works for Papa Bear might not work for Mama Bear or Baby Bear, but there is always going to be a "just right" fit for you if you're willing to search for it. There are several elements to consider when choosing how to structure your workplace environment. Always begin by thinking of your customer first. Their needs should be central to your model if you want to deliver the best customer experience. What does your customer need in terms of support? Will the customer benefit from in-person services? Can you improve your relationship by having someone available onsite?

The other big question to ask is: what services are you delivering? Does your offering require boots on the ground? For example, in some of the channels my company operates in, like managed IT practice, technicians do need to go onsite to assess and fix certain issues. Not everything is in the cloud, and technicians do need to go in person to data centers and server rooms, but the percentage of the work that needs to be done on-site is much lower than in the past. Still, even if the business does not require anyone to be onsite, I suggest a hybrid model because you want people in the office for collaboration, relationship building, and everything that goes along with that.

So, based on your customer needs and the services offered, you can create a work model that fits. Try to build in as much flexibility as you can (within reason) if you want to attract top talent. Allow your people to choose days that they can work from the office and days that they can work from home. Find the balance that puts your company in the right position to attract and retain top talent.

It may not be necessary for everyone to be in the office on the same day. You can structure the hybrid option, so certain teams meet in the office in order to meet specific business objectives. For example, if collaboration is a staple of your engineering team's problem-solving process, then make sure they have time and space to meet in person. You can choose one or two days a week when everyone is required to come to the office. "Setting clear goals and having a rhythm or process for measuring attainment against those goals is the biggest key to maintaining productivity in this new hybrid work model," says co-founder and M&A partner of the Evergreen Services Group, Ramsey Sahyoun. "It's important to set the tone that flexible work doesn't mean we have any less intensity on achieving our goals. If that is laid out clearly and there is a process around enforcing it, maintaining productivity becomes easy."

Finding the middle ground when it comes to your work model means that the employer will get their business objectives met by having everyone in the office as needed, and employees also get their desire for flexibility met. You can create a balance by understanding your business needs and your team members' needs and then creating a win-win strategy.

The Sticky Wicket

Now, you may be thinking that all sounds great, but Fred in accounting is never going to leave his cozy at-home setup. How do I convince employees who worked from home throughout the pandemic that there is real value—for them and for the company—in returning to the office? How do I motivate people to *want* to go back to face-to-face working, even on a hybrid model?

This is a really important question to address because some employees will be unwilling to return to in-person work, and even among those who agree to return, many may be unhappy about it—and an unhappy, unmotivated team is going to be less productive professionally. Consequently, their employee experience may trend toward the negative. We will dive into the answer in depth in the next chapter, but the bottom line is that you need to foster alignment among your staff.

This means that everyone on your team, throughout the organization, is on board with your company's mission and values, the cultural norms, and the workplace environment model. To achieve alignment, you have to understand who your people are and what they need. Work with team members who are having a hard time adjusting to help arrive at a solution that works for both of you. Try to meet their needs as well as your objectives.

Successful companies must have alignment across purpose, culture, and values; otherwise, the result will be discord and divergence. Unfortunately, if there is no alignment, then the only solution will likely be to find someone else who does align with your company's values and culture. If that sounds harsh, think of it this way: they want a certain freedom, and so do you. So, you make the choice to respect each other's freedoms. Sometimes that means finding a new team member who is aligned with your business objectives.

Different Industries, Different Needs

There is no one-size-fits-all solution when it comes to work models. Different industries will have different needs, and to complicate things further, different branches within an industry will also have different needs. So, let's look at some of the verticals and what the future workplace might look like for them.

Technology Service Providers. Technology Service Professionals can work remotely or on-site. So, a remote or hybrid work model will work for technical services teams and other functions such as Sales, Marketing, HR, and Finance. However, onsite technical services teams will collaborate better in the office by helping less-experienced engineers resolve tickets more efficiently, plus offer the flexibility to be dispatched directly from home to the customer site when needed.

Legal Services. With legal services, the same rule applies as what we have discussed above. Often, a hybrid model will work best for businesses in this industry, but of course, there are always exceptions. For instance, while your legal advisors may only need to be in the office two or three days a week, your building services team will still need to be onsite every day.

Medical Services. This one is a no-brainer. Even with all the advances in telemedicine, it stands to reason that doctors, nurses, and medical support staff must be onsite. Not only do they need to be there to perform vital physical examinations, assessments, and treatments, but there is also the element of medical privacy and record-keeping compliance to consider. Again, we must first think of the customers' needs. That said, people on your human resources team, administrators, or purchasing agents might benefit from a hybrid model.

Manufacturing. This industry may not be as straightforward as you think! Yes, the actual work of physical manufacturing will still need to be done in person, but this industry is changing rapidly. The more things are automated, the more a hybrid model starts to make sense. You may not immediately think of a blockchain developer when you think of manufacturing, but blockchain technology is increasingly being used in different industries, including this one—and those roles are suited to work-from-home options.

We cannot list every industry, obviously, but the point is that every industry and every business will have its own particular needs and interests. To simplify, it comes down to this: the majority of the white-collar jobs and knowledge-based jobs will be able to use and benefit from hybrid working models, and any job that requires a physical component will likely need to remain fully in person.

Unlocking the Secrets of Talent Marketing

The business problem with talent marketing lies in the disconnect between the evolving talent landscape and the traditional marketing strategies employed by many organizations. While businesses have adapted their marketing plans to attract and win customers in the post-pandemic era, they often overlook the need for a comprehensive talent marketing plan. Traditional approaches like job fairs, television ads, and newspaper ads are no longer as effective in reaching and engaging top talent.

The changing dynamics of the workforce, combined with the unique aspirations and expectations of the new generation, require businesses to rethink their talent marketing strategies. To attract these sought-after individuals, companies must go beyond traditional recruitment methods and embrace innovative approaches. This involves leveraging digital platforms, social media, employer branding, and personalized experiences to create a compelling employer value proposition. By understanding the preferences and motivations of the new generation of top talent, organizations can tailor their talent marketing efforts to stand out and attract the best candidates.

A strong employer brand should be developed and communicated effectively, showcasing the company's values, culture, and opportunities for growth. Engaging content, such as employee stories and testimonials, can help build an authentic and attractive brand image. Additionally, targeted recruitment campaigns and partnerships with educational institutions and industry influencers can expand the talent pool.

How to Lead in a Hybrid and Diverse World

In the aftermath of the pandemic, SMBs found themselves thrust into Talent Wars, which required them to expand their hiring efforts beyond local boundaries, seeking candidates nationally and even internationally. However, these SMBs faced a significant challenge: they lacked the necessary experience and know-how to effectively onboard and lead diverse remote teams. With this sudden shift occurring overnight, there was little opportunity to provide leaders with the training and support needed to navigate the complexities of managing remote and culturally diverse teams. Consequently, these businesses began to encounter issues related to company culture, employee engagement, and overall productivity. IT MSPs, for instance, have hired individuals from different parts of the country and internationally—all with differing values, politics, etc. The challenge is integrating all of them into one community by building a new way to create a cohesive virtual workforce.

So in the new talent landscape, the challenge lies in building a truly engaged community at work that embraces diverse workplace models (remote, hybrid, and in-person) and brings together employees from different countries and cultures. The problem stems from the limitations of traditional approaches that rely on physical interactions and shared spaces. The traditional methods of fostering camaraderie through water cooler conversations and team-building activities fall short when not everyone is physically present in the office. To overcome this, businesses can implement strategies such as

- Leadership training to lead remote and diverse teams.

- Fostering open and inclusive communication channels.

- Leveraging technology to facilitate virtual collaboration and connection.

- Organizing virtual and in-person team-building activities and social events.

- Promoting cultural awareness and sensitivity through cross-cultural collaboration and knowledge sharing.

Creating a sense of belonging, emphasizing shared values, and recognizing and celebrating individual contributions can further enhance community engagement and build a strong and cohesive work culture that transcends physical boundaries. Jen Zaroski at VC3 shares how she uses communication for engagement: "We've been really intentional in our communication with our people. And transparent. You build that trust. And with that comes true, powerful engagement. When they trust the leadership and direction of the company, and they understand it, then they're clear on how they're a part of a larger purpose, and that is very motivating."

Effective leadership training and clear communication play a crucial role in engaging and uniting the workforce and ensuring that the company culture remains strong and vibrant regardless of geographical or work-related differences. Brad Schow, VP of ConnectWise, strongly believes that you have to "learn to identify your leaders early and start to invest in them. Your business growth depends on how much you invest in your leadership."

Remote and hybrid work models give us one more thing to think about: leadership styles. When offices were fully in-person, the power of a leader was a physical presence every day. What happened when people were made to work from home during the pandemic was that people who did not necessarily have the right leadership skills were now in charge of managing people in a whole new and unfamiliar way. A lot of the transition to virtual work was conducted on a trial-and-error basis. There were communication lags, and Zoom filters went rogue. At times, the sudden thrust into remote work led to overcorrection, like high levels of scrutiny and monitoring.

This created a level of distrust between employer and employee. Employers and managers thought that people were not working enough, and employees felt they were working more than ever now that they were not commuting and did not have the social distractions of an office environment.

To be a successful leader in the new world of work, there has to be a level of trust and alignment across every level of your business. Leaders must develop new management and relationship-building strategies, and good leaders are doing it really well in a hybrid workplace. They focus on trusting people, providing increased role and goal clarity, and delegating work where it's needed. They are managing their results rather than managing activities. The aim is fruitful partnership and productivity.

As John C. Maxwell has written, leaders need to get away from being travel agents, namely, selling employees on a destination without any knowledge as to how to get there themselves. Instead, they need to shift to being tour guides, namely, giving a clear "road map" to employees and going on the journey together.

The Challenge Ahead

The evolution of work patterns began with the introduction of email and BlackBerries®, followed by the rise of online job searches through platforms like LinkedIn and Indeed. Gradually, remote work gained popularity, with some managers being allowed to work remotely one day a week. However, it was the pandemic that accelerated the adoption of remote work on a broad scale, prompting people to reevaluate their work-life balance in a whole new light. This shift in the balance of control was partly facilitated by technology, which brought both benefits and challenges.

Technology, in many ways, helped redistribute power—and that can be a good thing! However, it also led to certain drawbacks, including reduced oversight, weakened leadership, and a decline in employee motivation and productivity. In the upcoming chapter, we will delve into these issues and explore how the Talentpreneurial mindset and a robust talent framework can offer solutions to thrive in the new talent landscape.

5

Talent Operating System – A Framework for Building and Sustaining Top-Talent Teams

Business and Team Success...It Really Can Happen

Amid the rapid evolution of the business landscape fueled by technologies like AI, machine learning, blockchain, and automation, organizations encounter a daunting task: navigating the new talent landscape, encompassing diverse work models and a workforce spanning various cultures and countries, to thrive in the new environment. While businesses have readily embraced frameworks like Entrepreneurial Operating System® (EOS®), Scaling Up, or Objectives and Key Results (OKRs) to mature their overall operations, there is one critical area that often remains overlooked: the talent system.

The absence of an integrated talent system designed for the post-pandemic new talent landscape poses a major challenge for SMBs. While standalone employee surveys, engagement systems, performance management systems, and traditional HRIS may be in place, their lack of integration hinders the effectiveness of the talent system. SMBs need a comprehensive and cohesive solution to address the unique demands of the evolving talent environment and maximize their talent management capabilities.

Pre-COVID talent frameworks and systems have proven inadequate in adapting to the evolving talent landscape. Often treated as an afterthought, these systems were not designed to address the dynamic changes brought on by the pandemic. Many organizations have been reactive rather than proactive in recognizing the crucial role talent plays in driving business success.

According to Brad Schow, VP and Business Transformation Evangelist at Connectwise, "Leading high-growth IT services companies (empire builders) require a talent system. It's critical—I can't stress that enough. It is crucial to implement a mature talent system."

I firmly believe that great entrepreneurs are Talentpreneurs first. I draw upon my twenty years of Talentpreneurial and CEO experience in building a global tech company that helps over 400 Technology Solution Providers (TSPs, also known as MSPs) with their tech talent needs. Talent should be at the forefront of every organization's strategy, and thus, the adoption of a comprehensive talent framework is imperative. This chapter aims to explore the crucial components of TOS to help you understand how you can apply this system to your business.

TOS: A Blueprint for Business and Team Success

I refer to this modern framework as a Talent Operating System (TOS). By embracing this blueprint, businesses can establish a winning talent strategy for attracting, hiring, engaging, aligning, and retaining top talent, leading to a scalable and self-transforming business in a fast-paced world. It expands beyond traditional HR practices by empowering organizations to create a culture of excellence where innovation thrives—and teams become unstoppable forces.

It allows leaders to seamlessly align business vision, strategy, and goals with talent strategy, ensuring that every aspect of the organization is optimized for peak performance. With its arsenal of simple yet powerful tools and processes, TOS enables Talentpreneurs to build thriving businesses and lives, unlocking the true potential of their teams and paving the way for a scalable and self-transforming future.

The TOS Framework

With its five success strategies, TOS empowers entrepreneurs and leaders to achieve business success through Talentpreneurship. Leaders can use this framework to build a rock-solid team that continuously transforms their business and life. From strategic alignment and workforce analysis to training, succession planning, and performance management, TOS equips SMBs with the tools to optimize their talent and achieve remarkable business outcomes in the new talent landscape.

1. **Business Strategy:** Your strategic alignment begins with defining a clear purpose, vision, long-term and

short-term goals, and strategic objectives. You can use a business operating system such as EOS, Scaling Up, and OKRs to define your business strategy. Identify how workforce planning aligns with and supports these goals. Ensure the workforce plan is integrated with the overall business strategy. For example, if you are a technology solutions provider and your goal is 25% annual growth, you can create a workforce forecast for remote and onsite engineers, service and account managers, and other roles required to accommodate growth without compromising brand reputation and customer and employee experience.

2. **Talent Strategy:** Talent planning is a critical process that involves a comprehensive analysis to identify key roles and skills required to align with your business strategy. Begin by conducting a thorough talent review of your current workforce. Evaluate various aspects such as employee culture alignment, career aspirations, unique strengths, passion, demographics, skills, competencies, experience, and performance.

   Maintain an early warning list to detect potential culture misalignment, skills gaps, and mismatches in passion and talents. Use the insights from this analysis to conduct a talent mapping exercise, aligning the findings with your present workforce needs. Additionally, plan for the future by forecasting workforce requirements based on sales projections, the sales pipeline, new client onboarding timelines, and strategic objectives. Anticipate technological advancements, industry trends, and market demands to stay ahead.

Identify the number of employees, roles, and skills needed to meet future demands, considering factors like attrition, promotions, retirements, and new positions. As the final step, implement a succession planning strategy. Review your workforce analysis and future workforce plan to pinpoint key positions requiring succession planning. Identify high-potential employees for future roles and establish career development, learning paths, and mentoring programs to promote internal growth. Ensure a seamless transition for critical roles to maintain business continuity. Popular succession planning tools like The Nine-Box Grid can be utilized to assess employees based on their performance and potential.

With a clear understanding of your talent needs and preferences, you're poised to develop a 12-month talent forecast. To attract top talent, it's essential to devise robust talent marketing strategies, an area often overlooked by small businesses in contrast to client marketing. Start by outlining targeted candidate profiles and crafting specific job ads for each position. Embrace diverse sourcing avenues, such as referrals, job boards, and professional networks, and consider tapping into the global talent pool for remote positions. Enhance your appeal by cultivating a strong employer brand and workplace culture. Additionally, consider setting up an alumni network for former employees and a "golden ticket" program to welcome back standout professionals.

3. **Culture & Community:** As a leader, know your core values and engage your team in co-creating a

culture plan. Base all business decisions on these values, from hiring to firing and rewards. Foster a collaborative environment supported by a dedicated culture team. Embrace mindsets of positivity, growth, life-long learning, and entrepreneurial thinking to make big choices for innovation. Prioritize clarity, trust, and communication for team rapport. Create a true sense of community at work by cultivating connection, belonging, and purpose. We will elaborate on this in the next chapter.

The second part of this is cross-functional communication, collaboration, and transparency. Here you must get buy-in from the key cross-functional leaders and create a collaborative environment for effective teamwork with a high level of accountability standards to execute well on the talent plan. Clearly communicate the talent strategy and outcomes to key leaders and employees. Foster open lines of communication to address concerns and feedback. Provide regular updates on progress and outcomes. Remember, the key to a successful annual talent plan is its flexibility and adaptability to meet the changing needs of your business. Regularly review and adjust the plan as necessary, leveraging feedback and data-driven insights for continuous improvement.

Engagement and employee experience are critical components to build a strong culture and community. In the remote and hybrid workplace, true employee engagement holds greater significance than ever before. It fuels productivity, aligns individuals with business goals, and fosters top talent retention. By nurturing a sense of belonging, connection, purpose, recognition, and a rewards system, organizations can build a community at work to unleash the full team potential and drive remarkable business outcomes in the new work environment. We will discuss more on this topic in the coming chapters.

4. **Continuous Transformation:** Foster a culture of continuous transformation through regular review and learning. You are learning or winning by regularly reviewing what's working and not working. As your team is learning and winning, it is essential that you provide coaching, mentoring, and guidance for continuous performance transformation. With the rise of remote and hybrid work models, it is crucial to have an effective performance management process for your team and business success. Traditional annual performance reviews do not produce the best results in the distributed workforce model. Continuous performance management focuses on ongoing performance discussions, feedback, and coaching rather than just annual performance reviews. It promotes regular communication between managers and employees, setting clear goals, providing timely feedback, and fostering accountability, leading to enhanced productivity, alignment, job satisfaction, and top talent retention.

Ramsey Sahyoun, co-founder and M&A partner of Evergreen Services Group says, "Setting clear goals and having a rhythm or process for measuring attainment against those goals is the biggest key to maintaining productivity in this new hybrid work model. I think it's important to set the tone that flexible work doesn't mean we have any less intensity on achieving our goals. If that is laid out clearly and there is a process around enforcing it, maintaining productivity becomes easy." In the next chapter, we will discuss the performance management framework and best practices in detail.

Continuous learning and development are key for continuous transformation. Invest in your people. Create a robust training and development program to enhance employee skills. Provide ongoing learning opportunities to close the skills gap and foster career growth. Promote from within to feed your future workforce plan and retention objectives. Identify relevant training resources, including internal and external options. A lot of vendors, such as technology companies and industry associations, have MDF funds or scholarship programs to train your employees. Encourage continuous learning and skill-building among employees and send them to industry conferences to learn industry trends and future predictions.

5. **Compliance and Quality Assurance:** Implementing quality controls is crucial to ensure the effectiveness of best practices for attracting, hiring, developing, engaging, and retaining top talent. Without these controls, your talent strategy may falter and fail to yield consistent results. As you manage people, it's imperative to remain legally compliant and consistently educate your team on evolving HR regulations.

TOS®| TALENT OPERATING SYSTEM

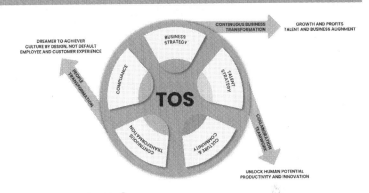

TALENTPRENEURSHIP™

The TOS provides a comprehensive framework for SMBs to build top-talent teams that deliver remarkable business outcomes. By aligning talent strategy with business goals, fostering a culture of excellence, and continuously optimizing talent management practices, organizations can thrive in the new talent landscape. Embracing TOS is the key to creating a scalable and self-transforming business that stays ahead in a rapidly evolving world.

In the upcoming chapters, we will delve deeper into key components of the TOS framework, including Vision, Culture, Community, Purpose, Performance Management, Talent Acquisition, Talent Mapping, Entrepreneurial Thinking, and Employee Experience.

6

Entrepreneurial Success Through TOS

Great Entrepreneurs Are Talentpreneurs First

I n the previous chapter, we explored the concept of TOS and its significance for entrepreneurs. Building upon that, this chapter delves deeper into the key elements of being a successful Talentpreneur. It emphasizes the importance of proactive efforts in cultivating and sustaining high-performance teams, which ultimately leads to sustainable growth and competitive advantage.

Throughout this chapter, we will explore various aspects critical to talent optimization. We begin by discussing the role of culture in creating an environment conducive to high performance. We then move on to best practices for developing a hiring process that is future-proof and aligned with the evolving talent landscape. Additionally, we explore strategies for achieving performance excellence, aligning individual strengths with the company's vision and talent requirements, and fostering both entrepreneurial and Talentpreneurial thinking within the team.

By unlocking creative thinking, seizing opportunities, and driving innovation through effective teamwork, leaders can position their organization for success in the face of constant change. This chapter serves as a call to action, urging leaders to adopt continuous transformation in their talent strategies. This approach ensures that the organization's workforce remains future-ready and empowers them to achieve their goals.

The Foundation of TOS: Culture

As Peter Drucker famously stated, "Culture eats strategy for breakfast." This quote underscores the vital role that culture plays in an organization's success. No matter how well-crafted your business strategy may be, it will falter without a strong and aligned culture. To build and sustain this culture, understanding and consistently communicating your core values is imperative.

As a leader, it is essential to embody the values you wish to instill in your team. "People may teach what they know, but they reproduce what they are," as leadership author John Maxwell has said. Your actions and behaviors as a leader will attract individuals with whom your values resonate. By consistently living your values, you inspire others to do the same. Jake Spanberger, CEO of Entech, Florida-based PE-backed IT Services Company, shares that "our five core values are: we do what's right; we win as a team; we figure it out; we grow, or we die; and we build and value great relationships. That's the number, the five tenets of who we are as a company. Everything that we do, all the shared services, all the corporate-level initiatives, all starts with those five principles in mind. However, the individual who runs a particular geography, who runs that particular location, has to mold their culture into their own vision because they're the ones who are driving it."

For continuous culture transformation, involve your talent leader and a group of dedicated volunteers, known as culture ambassadors, to co-create and lead your culture plan. Establish employee feedback mechanisms to gain insights into what is working and what needs improvement. Incorporate culture progress reports into all internal corporate communications, such as team meetings, newsletters, town halls, and state-of-the-company updates. By focusing on building a strong company culture, you lay the foundation for success, driving innovation and creating a thriving and engaged workforce.

CBD | CULTURE BY DESIGN

THE FIVE Cs FORMULA

It Takes a Village: Great Talentpreneurs Build Healthy Communities

Let's explore strategies for building a strong community at work that empowers people and drives your business forward. Leading Talentpreneurs understand the importance of building a true community at work, just like a village. They recognize that it takes a village to grow a successful business. They create a healthy community where talented individuals come together with a shared sense of purpose. By fostering a culture of collaboration, support, and belonging, they empower their team members to self-manage and contribute to a profitable business with clearly defined outcomes.

Every Truly Effective Community Has a Well-Defined Purpose

Exceptional leaders can bring about transformative changes in organizations by going beyond simple business goals and creating a strong sense of purpose. They understand that an organization driven by a meaningful purpose not only achieves remarkable success but also fosters a genuine sense of community among its members. To establish such an organization, leaders must define a compelling purpose that resonates with employees, customers, and stakeholders alike.

This purpose serves as a unifying force, attracting individuals who seek a deeper meaning in their work and inspiring everyone to work towards a shared objective. In particular, Millennials and Gen Z employees actively seek employers whose purpose aligns with their personal values, desiring a sense of belonging and a community-oriented environment.

By nurturing a purpose that goes beyond mere profits, leaders can create a workplace where individuals feel connected, motivated, and part of something greater than themselves. When leaders align their strategies, culture, and actions with this purpose, they can establish a business that prioritizes belonging—where motivation, fulfillment, and a true sense of community flourish. The true essence of business lies in building purpose-driven organizations that cultivate a genuine sense of community in the workplace.

From Vision to Victory: Talentpreneurs Are Great Visionaries

Great leaders understand the power of a compelling vision in driving organizational success. They craft a clear and inspiring business vision that captures the essence of what the organization aspires to become. However, they don't stop there. These leaders go above and beyond by effectively communicating and gaining team buy-in for the vision. By engaging and involving team members in the vision-setting process, they create a shared sense of ownership and commitment. With everyone aligned and driven by a common purpose, the team becomes unstoppable, executing the vision and turning it into a reality.

The Power of Alignment: Vision, Strategy, Goals, and Scorecards

Let's now elaborate on the continuous performance management strategy discussed in the previous chapter on TOS. Continuous performance management starts with having a crystal-clear business vision, strategy, goals, and company scorecard. Jack Daly, Amazon best-selling author and CEO of Professional Sales Coach, says, "When I'm asking business owners what their vision is, what I'm trying to get is an understanding of what it is they're attempting to build. What does the company look like in the future, whether it's five years out or ten years out? You can't get there unless you know what there is. So, I can't begin to help a CEO or a business owner until I understand what the definition of success is, what the destination is."

To align all company assets in one direction and measure progress, you can use performance management planning tools and frameworks such as a Balanced Scorecard (BSC). The BSC is a strategic performance management framework that translates an organization's strategy into a set of balanced objectives and performance measures across four domains: financial, customer, internal processes, and learning and growth.

These scorecards become your compass, highlighting the crucial numbers that truly matter: aspects like culture, revenues, profits, customer retention, percentage of top talent, retention, employee and customer experience, and innovation. With this comprehensive approach, clarity and alignment become second nature across all facets of your business.

As a leader, you must inspect what you expect. The company scorecard serves as your true north, outlining strategic objectives, financial targets, customer satisfaction goals, operational efficiencies, and other critical metrics that define your triumph. By painting a vivid picture of what needs to be achieved and the actions required to get there, the scorecard fosters shared understanding and accountability. It becomes your go-to reference point for decision-making, allowing you to evaluate progress, identify gaps, and pivot when necessary to stay on the path to victory.

At IT By Design, we believe in forging an unbreakable connection throughout the organization. To make this happen, we craft departmental scorecards that breathe life into the grand strategy, breaking it down into specific objectives and targets for each functional area. This cascading approach empowers every department with a deep understanding of its crucial role in achieving the company's lofty goals. With crystal-clear expectations and measurable targets in place, these scorecards fuel focused execution, accountability, and diligent performance tracking.

It's about creating a powerful line of sight where all team member's efforts are directly linked to the department's outcomes. This connection ignites a passionate drive within each individual, knowing that their contributions matter and make a difference. It's this unwavering synergy that propels us toward the pinnacle of organizational triumph. Together, we rise, achieve, and surpass our wildest dreams.

And it doesn't end with departments. We recognize the value of each individual and their role in your company's triumph. Individual scorecards are crafted to align employee goals with broader organizational objectives. These scorecards define key performance indicators and targets for each employee, establishing clear expectations and nurturing a sense of ownership. By connecting individual aspirations to the larger strategic framework, employees gain a profound understanding of how their work directly impacts the company's success. This alignment fuels engagement, motivation, and a shared sense of purpose among your talented workforce.

But we don't stop there, either. We focus further on the employee experience scorecard, building a positive work environment that attracts, retains, and develops top talent. Measuring aspects like employee satisfaction, engagement, career growth opportunities, and work-life balance, we monitor and enhance the factors that drive employee well-being. We foster a culture of continuous improvement and create a virtuous cycle where happy employees translate into happy customers. Employee referrals and customer satisfaction soar, propelling your organization to new heights.

Equally important is the customer experience scorecard, which evaluates your ability to deliver exceptional customer service and meet customer expectations. By measuring customer satisfaction, retention, loyalty, and overall customer experience, you can continuously refine your approach to exceed expectations. A customer-centric focus builds trust, fosters long-lasting relationships, and generates referable business growth.

Lastly, we delve into the innovation scorecard, assessing your organization's ability to foster a culture of innovation, adapt to market dynamics, and drive continuous improvement. By tracking metrics related to research and development, new product/service development, process innovation, and the implementation of innovative ideas, you stay one step ahead of the competition. Embracing innovation enables you to identify new growth opportunities and become an industry leader, especially as we navigate the upcoming AI revolution.

The power of a clear business strategy, goals, and a comprehensive scorecard cannot be overstated. It provides the compass that guides your organization to success, aligns every aspect of your business, and enables effective decision-making. By weaving together department scorecards, individual scorecards, employee experience scorecards, customer experience scorecards, and innovation scorecards, you foster alignment, accountability, and a sense of purpose at every level. This holistic approach creates a rock-solid foundation for achieving strategic objectives, delivering exceptional customer experiences, and cultivating a thriving, innovative, and victorious organizational culture.

Talent Acquisition

These strategies are integral to fueling your success through TOS, ensuring that your organization can cultivate an authentic culture with clear branding, evolving hiring strategies, and talent development that will keep your employees engaged and motivated.

Employer Branding: Build a strong and appealing employer brand that showcases your organization's values, culture, and benefits. Highlight the unique aspects of your workplace and communicate them effectively through various channels, such as social media, career websites, and employee testimonials. Engage your employees to create career educational video content to attract like-minded applicants. For example, for our employer branding, I have a podcast called "Career and Culture Corner" to interview our employees and share their growth journey and career experiences. We share this educational video content for professionals on all social media and podcast platforms to build online talent communities that improve our time-to-hire by sourcing candidates from our online community.

Digital Recruitment: Leverage digital platforms and technology to expand your reach and attract top talent. Utilize online job boards, professional networking sites, and social media platforms to engage with potential candidates and promote job opportunities effectively. Use digital platforms to host virtual job fairs. We have a weekly virtual "meet and greet" group info session for new candidates to learn about the company culture and open roles.

Remote and Flexible Work Options: Embrace the shift towards remote and flexible work arrangements. Highlight the flexibility and work-life harmony your organization offers to attract top talent seeking a better work-life integration. Embrace global talent strategies for fast and cost-effective labor for appropriate remote roles.

Skills-based Hiring: Move away from traditional credentials-based hiring and focus on assessing candidates based on their skills and potential. Implement skill-based assessments and consider alternative qualifications that may indicate a candidate's ability to excel in the role.

Employee Referral Programs: Encourage your existing employees to refer talented individuals they know. Implement a robust employee referral program that rewards employees for successful referrals. Existing employees can be valuable sources for identifying top talent. Implement an employee recognition and rewards program to promote referrals. We recognize employees with the highest referrals during our quarterly awards ceremony.

Data-driven Recruitment: Utilize data and analytics to monitor and manage your recruitment strategies. Analyze recruitment metrics, track the effectiveness of different sourcing channels, and leverage data-driven insights to optimize your talent acquisition efforts. Create a list of recruitment strategy success measures such as cost-per-hire, top-talent hires, etc.

Talent Pipeline Development: Create and nurture a talent pipeline to proactively build relationships with potential candidates. Engage with talent communities, industry events, and educational institutions to identify and connect with promising individuals who may be a good fit for future roles. Create collaborations with talent partners (staffing partners such as IT By Design for MSP talent) in your niche to source quality talent.

Talent Alumni Community: Create an alumni program for employees with rehire status. Give your top talent a golden ticket during their exit and encourage them to return if the grass is not greener on the other side and they want to return to water their old grass. Engage them by including them in your company newsletter and social and charity events. Add your open positions in the newsletter and invite them to apply for open positions. At IT By Design, we invite them to our social events, give back activities, and allow them to join our online wellness program.

By implementing these talent acquisition and recruitment strategies, you can position your organization to acquire top talent in the post-pandemic talent landscape. Remember to adapt and evolve your strategies as the talent landscape continues to evolve.

7

Building an Unstoppable Team

Be a Superhero and Think like an Entrepreneur

To create distinct value for your customers and build a self-managed, recession-proof business, it's crucial to align your team's strengths with the company's vision and encourage entrepreneurial thinking. In this chapter, we discuss the power of entrepreneurial team thinking and aligning unique individual strengths with business needs and wants. By understanding your team members' unique strengths and passions, you can successfully leverage their "superpowers," leading to superior results.

Aligning Your Team's Strengths with the Company's Vision

It's your responsibility as a thoughtful employer to help people discover their "superpower"—their strengths, their passions, and what's energizing for them. As a result, you will be co-creating that alignment with the business tasks that need to be completed, only now the people accomplishing those goals will feel aligned with the activity. It is invigorating both for them and for the company. Still, it takes time and effort—and yes, a bit of your budget—to achieve alignment. So, what makes this an investment and not a cost? What is your cost of misaligned talent? What is your return on investment for helping your employees feel fulfilled in their work and invested in your vision? How do you measure those results?

The long and short of it is this: the results of alignment are higher productivity, better employee satisfaction, longer retention of top talent, improved financial performance, and superior customer experience. These are all goals that you should be aiming for.

YOU
VISION & CULTURE
LEVERAGE YOUR STRENGTHS
OUTSOURCE YOUR WEAKNESSES

TEAM
VISION ALIGNMENT
COMPLEMENTARY STRENGTHS
CAREER BLUEPRINT

TALENT

YOUR
VALUE OFFERING

BUSINESS STRATEGY
TALENT STRATEGY
TALENT PLATFORM

TOOLS

TRAINING

TECHNICAL
PROCESS
LEADERSHIP

T^3
TALENTPRENEURSHIP™

Your Own Team of Superheroes

The first step in achieving alignment throughout your team is identifying each person's "superpower." Knowing each person's unique strength can help you empower and develop them to make better contributions to the company. As Jim Collins, author of *Good to Great*, put it, "You have the right people on the bus; now you have to make sure they're in the right seat."

Start by assessing each team member's strengths and areas for improvement. There are a number of simple steps you can take to make your initial assessment and adjust it as you progress in the role. You can use a combination of one-on-one meetings, surveys, assessments, and feedback from colleagues and customers to determine their primary strengths and how they might stand out from other members of their team. Have an open and honest conversation about their career goals, aspirations, and interests. Ask them what they enjoy doing and what they feel they are best at.

Next, compare that information to the goals of your company. How will that person best serve the mission and vision? What can you do to align them with that vision? Analyze the controls and responsibilities of each team member, consider the future needs of the team and the organization, and then think about what skills and experiences will be required to fulfill those needs and achieve those goals. Work with each team member to develop a career development plan, including future opportunities for each team member.

It is also important to review each team member's progress regularly and adjust the career development plan as necessary. Encourage feedback from team members, and then celebrate successes and recognize achievements. It's all about emphasizing positive achievements and encouraging your people.

That all sounds great, right? But what does that look like in real terms? For example, a chief technology officer (CTO) may discover that he is a lot more effective when it comes to technical problem-solving rather than the management and people side of the role, where his strength lies in looking at a problem and knowing exactly what technology or process will solve it. That is what he enjoys, and that is what energizes him. So, structure his career development plan around opportunities that suit that strength, foster his growth, and benefit the company because then you will have your best person contributing solutions to your most difficult technology problems.

As another example, a VP of Strategy and Transformation may uncover that his superpower is knowing and managing numbers. His talent can be positioned to lead the most important numbers in the company scorecard.

It is possible in both these examples that they—and we as leaders—would never have known that they had these natural gifts or that they were applicable in the workplace had we not gone through the process of discovering them (thanks to Strategic Coach Unique Ability Workshop). We hired a Strategic Coach® team to help our leadership team discover their Unique Ability®. It is a huge win for both the company and your team members to go through this process because there is a lot of friction between result and effort when someone is not doing Unique Ability work.

I will give you one more example of what I mean by this. We had someone in the role of Operations Manager. He enjoyed operations, and we thought he suited the role. He was a great human being and a hard worker. But there was always friction with scorecard results. We could not understand what was happening. He was putting in a ton of effort but not delivering the corresponding results. He was stressed out all the time, and the people working around him were frustrated, as well. He was on the road to burning out, and he was costing the company valuable time and money by not performing at the level expected for that role.

We decided to work through the process of finding his superpower and discovered that operations was not it. That was where the friction was. He was much more suited to the people side of the business. We switched him from operations to talent building. He started to shine. Right away, he started producing results in terms of team building, recruitment, training, and retention because now he was using his god-gifted talents.

When someone is working within their Unique Ability, the effort required to produce excellent results is drastically minimized. It reduces friction. If they are skilled at what they're doing and they are energized by it, you are going to see performance and productivity skyrocket.

A Cascade of Happiness and Results

When a person is doing unique ability work, they are happier with themselves, more confident, and more productive. They go home happy. And the company is happy because they are getting the right contributions and results. They are able to hit the numbers or success criteria that they are supposed to hit. They're getting the best value out of their investment in their talent. And the team as a whole is happy because it feels satisfying to achieve amazing results together. It's an all-around win.

The best thing you can do to grow your company is to invest in the growth of your people. The data is clear, "The most important part of [talent management] is to never stop thinking about your employees' potential and talent. No other factor is likely to make such a big difference when it comes to building a high-performing team."[8]

When you invest in a person as an individual, it is exactly that—an investment. They get to grow and develop as individuals but also in whatever their role is for the company. Their sense of fulfillment will motivate them to keep performing at their best. The individual is happy, the team is happy, as are the company, the stakeholders, and your customers. And that means your numbers are going to be great, which will make your CFO happy, too! What more could you want?

It may sound trite, but a big part of what I love about running my business the way I do is that I believe we are creating happiness. What else is there in life?

What Is the Cost of Happiness?

It is all well and good to say that an investment in your talent is an investment in your company and its future, but what does that mean in reality? What is the bottom line when it comes to happiness? For instance, what is the cost of putting somebody through a Kolbe assessment or The Strategic Coach Program? How big a check do you have to write to do this?

Most of the popular assessment tools will run you less than one hundred dollars per person; some online versions are as little as twenty. On the upper end, you might spend $250 on a qualified specialist for members of your leadership or executive team. Additionally, the conversations and career planning can be done in large part directly with the team members' managers, leadership, or even your HR manager or specialist.

In the grand scheme of things, that cost is going to be much lower than whatever it would cost you if you *don't* find out the superpowers of your talent. Don't underestimate the hidden cost of underperforming employees. That cost will be significantly higher than the assessment or the value of someone performing at their best by doing unique ability work on a regular basis.

As one business improvement expert put it, "Even good people can go off the rails when they don't have clear roles and goals. So, imagine what happens if poor performers don't have clear roles and goals."[9] There are hidden costs to this as well, to the individual, their team, and the company. "It's not just the damage caused externally to customer relationships through poor work. It's the massive damage done internally to the trust between owners/managers and their staff."[10]

It is easy to imagine the kind of damage that can be done by underperforming employees—to morale, to customer relationships, and to your company's overall success. You might lose good people or valuable customers if you have people in the wrong roles. And that damage can be hard to undo.

Yes, there is an upfront cost for some of the tools that will help you uncover your team members' superpowers, but that investment will save you a lot in the long term. It will save you money, and it will improve your relationships with other employees and your customers.

You might still be thinking, well, I have fifty employees, and at a hundred bucks a pop, that is going to cost me five thousand dollars! For that money, you want to ensure you get a meaningful return on investment.

In the competitive landscape of attracting the best talent, investing in your people becomes the most valuable strategy, especially in professional services industries. This approach is backed by solid evidence. According to *Harvard Business Review*, "We could improve productivity if we stopped systematically underinvesting in human capital."[11] They go on to say that one of the best ways to invest in your people is through training and talent development, "Beyond wages, other forms of investment in human capital include education and training… [and] the time and space to explore new ideas and professional development opportunities."

Investing in your people and finding their superpowers is one of the secrets of success among top-performing companies. In a broad study, research showed that "The top-quartile companies in our study unlocked 40% more productive power in their workforce through better practices in time, talent, and energy management."[12]

This creates a cascade effect. If you invest in your people, they will produce better results, and those results get them to reinvest in your mission and goals and increase their alignment, which increases the value they are able to produce on behalf of your company. Collectively, every action is being completed with a high degree of quality and care, which creates value for the company.

To tie in some of what we discussed in the previous chapter, creating a great company culture and having alignment within your team is also a great way to attract and retain younger talent. We know that Millennials and Generation Zers ("Zoomers") want to work for companies that give them a sense of purpose and that they feel are making the world a better place. Younger workers want to feel seen, and there is no better way of doing that than by helping them identify and nurture their unique abilities.

The takeaway is this: finding your talent's unique abilities and developing those people further creates happiness, energy, alignment, and greater ROI. Most importantly, it will help you build a great culture, one founded on personal fulfillment and alignment with your company's vision. It is a way to transform lives.

In the next chapter, we are going to take this practice one step further. We will take a deeper dive into developing your top talent by empowering and educating them to think like entrepreneurs because the highest-performing companies out there are the ones with entrepreneurial thinkers on their teams.

Encouraging Entrepreneurial Thinking with Everyone on Your Team

Education, life-long learning, new thinking, winning and learning, and continuous transformation are important mindsets at my company. This is crucial not only because companies perform better when their team members are entrepreneurial thinkers, but it is also important to retain growth mindset talent.

That is what Life By Design is all about. You might be the greatest mind in your line of business, but how do you impart your business acumen to your team members? At IT By Design, we appreciate The Experience Transformer® from Strategic Coach (available at www.StrategicCoach. com), and we share lots of tools to help develop our team members' thinking. Most of all, we make it okay for them to fail. The biggest source of resistance to entrepreneurial thinking is this: "If I fail, I'll be judged."

So, in this chapter, we'll discuss easy-to-implement options to dramatically increase the level of entrepreneurial thinking in your company.

Cut Through the Red Tape

You may not think that everyone on your team needs to think the way you do or have the same entrepreneurial mindset. Does your salesperson really need to be thinking about the company's big picture? Does the tech engineer need to be thinking about your end-of-year goals? Yes! It may seem counterintuitive, but when everyone can think like an entrepreneur, then everyone feels helpful and productive.

Everyone wants to avoid feeling restricted or trapped in bureaucratic bottlenecks. When you have successfully attracted top talent, they are eager to excel, not only for your organization's benefit but also for their personal growth. This mindset of thinking like an entrepreneur, supported by proper education and training, is especially vital for supervisors, team leads, managers, and leadership roles. By cultivating this entrepreneurial thinking, you empower your team to be proactive, innovative, and better equipped to handle challenges, ultimately driving the success of your organization and personal advancement.

The pace of the world that we live in is faster than ever before. If your standard operating procedures or chain of communication can't keep up, if the speed of decision-making is slowed down because of the bureaucratic layers in your organization, your business is going to fall behind. Having a team that can think entrepreneurially also means you remove a lot of the bureaucratic red tape.

You can cut out layer upon layer of decision-makers when you trust your team from top to bottom, knowing that they have the same business acumen, values, and foresight. That means no more waiting for each link in the chain to approve a change or process; your business can operate light and fast, making you more efficient overall. The speed of your team really depends on the speed of the structure. The last thing you want for your business is for another company to take a competing product to the market, offering a better customer experience before you can.

For example, the Four Seasons powerhouse hotel organization is a great example of how and why this works. They empower every employee to create a top-tier experience for all their guests. As they say, "We know that the best way to enable our people to deliver these exceptional guest experiences is through a world-class employee experience and company culture... We support personal growth through structured training and continued career development..."[13] They allocate a monthly budget for this express purpose. As long as their team can put a smile on someone's face and create a positive experience, then that expense is worthwhile.

On the flip side, their competitors might have to go through a long process to deliver the same outcome. If a team member is on a call with a guest, they may need to loop in their account managers and customer success manager. Everything would need to be reviewed and approved. The whole customer experience is forced to slow down. Additionally, with more managerial layers needed for approval, your burden weight goes up. Financially speaking, this increases your costs and decreases profits. That, in turn, decreases the valuation of the company because your EBITDA is not high.

Ultimately, the way you structure your organization and empower your people has an impact on your finances, customer experience, and employee satisfaction. In today's technologically advanced and fast-paced environment, you want your employees to go out there and be competitive.

By empowering and educating your whole team, you can set the standard for your industry and take on a leadership role. By creating a workplace environment that is entrepreneurial—rather than bureaucratic or corporate—you are creating a model of success that no one else can top. Sounds great, right? So how do you get you *and* your team to the top spot?

Everything Starts with Education

Creating a culture of entrepreneurship is a way of life, a way of thinking, and a way of acting. It is a journey, not an event. So, let's first take a step back. To begin, there are a lot of simple things that you can do during the screening and hiring process to make sure you're building the best team from the get-go.

Set criteria during the interview process that will help determine whether your potential candidates are entrepreneurially minded. Ask questions about their past employment history and the results they were able to achieve. Was there a time they were able to think outside the box to solve a difficult problem? Then, ask them what they would do differently next time so the problem is solved better, faster, or cheaper. Were they able to take a low-value asset and make it a high-value asset? Find out if growth and development are important values to them.

Maybe they haven't had the opportunity to work in an entrepreneurial environment, but they are capable of thinking like an entrepreneur. An entrepreneur is someone who creates value. That's who you want to hire.

Then, during the training for new hires, make sure your boot camp or orientation program encourages people towards education, continued training, and professional coaching. For existing employees, implement a strategy to deliver on that promise of continued training. Drive home why it is important—explain the benefits to both employee and customer experience and the overall financial performance of the company.

With your training and education strategy in place, you can implement assessments. We use a version of a scorecard, for example, which tracks the key performance indicators (KPIs) of our team members. This helps measure and manage the entrepreneurial health of the team members. To this end, we do quarterly "alignment calls," when we review the scorecard of KPIs of the individual, including entrepreneurial thinking. We review each team member's job description and career development plan, and we use that to evaluate their KPIs. Based on this, they receive a performance rating to help keep them on track.

How you go about this will depend on the size and structure of your business. If you run a small business, you may not have an internal trainer, in which case, you will need to partner up with one. Most SMBs will have a human resources manager, so if you don't have a special training manager, then you can use your HR manager.

In addition to this, anyone in a leadership role—meaning anyone with a people management role—should dedicate a significant amount of time to coaching and training their team. It should be in every manager's KPIs to do a certain number of training hours per month with their team. Again, depending on the size of your business, the lead role might be taken by one person—the CEO or HR manager—or if you run a bigger company, you might have a whole training division with a learning and development manager who can take the lead.

Tools of the Trade

Some of the simplest tools are the best. Create a Microsoft PowerPoint presentation that includes the content and tools that you want to teach, and then train managers to do that within their respective divisions. If you are the one developing this material, you first have to define the entrepreneurial environment and culture. An oft-cited definition by economist Jean Baptiste is that an entrepreneur is someone who shifts economic resources out of an area of lower productivity and into an area of higher productivity and greater yield. Alongside this, be sure to include examples of the behaviors you want to create and what you want to educate people on to develop that entrepreneurial environment.

What are the success criteria for creating an entrepreneurial culture? This will look different for different segments of your business. For example, how might a salesperson think like an entrepreneur? They would need to know what kinds of questions to ask to determine the best way to create value for the customer. If they can understand the customer and what they want in terms of value, then they can deliver above and beyond what the customer has asked for. They are thinking like an entrepreneur and *adding* value to the customer experience.

However, someone on your finance team will create value in a different way. A CFO or controller can be an entrepreneurial thinker by looking at the valuation of the company. Whether you run a privately held business or a publicly traded company, you should be thinking about your potential shareholders and stakeholders. If their share value is one dollar, then the CFO needs to think about how to turn that into ten dollars over the next three years—even if they aren't reporting to a board. This is entrepreneurial thinking.

The same goes for the customer service arm of your company. When your customer service team interacts with customers, they should try to deliver more value for that customer than what the company receives in payment. Educate your people at every level about entrepreneurship, and you will see the benefits across every branch of your business.

It is also important to keep the flow of communication and ideas moving. At IT By Design, we have a learning lunch every Friday where managers take turns developing content for the upcoming company training session, which always includes a segment on how to foster entrepreneurial thinking.

We also do a bigger and more intensive quarterly training. This is a full day devoted to looking at where each manager is in terms of their journey, training their team members, and the resources they have to do this. These are just a few of the ways to foster entrepreneurship throughout your team.

Failing Upwards

At the heart of entrepreneurship is the willingness and courage to take risks. And risk-taking—even strategic, managed risks—means that sometimes you will fail. Now, a common response to failure in business is criticism, performance improvement plans, loss of bonuses, and sometimes it can even lead to termination. That can really take a sledgehammer to employee morale. It can make them less entrepreneurial (risk-averse), and their Monday morning, well, suck.

I would urge you to take an alternative route when your employees fail. At my company, we have created a culture where it is okay to fail. Now, this isn't a carte blanche, but it is important to give employees a safe space to try different ways of operating. (And safety is right there at the foundation of Maslow's Hierarchy of Needs.) That is how you drive innovation.

When you empower your employees to think outside the box and embrace new challenges, they might encounter failures along the way. But let me tell you, it's in those daring moments that they discover brilliant ways to improve, innovate, and achieve greatness. They'll astonish you with their creativity and determination, finding ways to do things better, faster, and more cost-effectively.

And you know what happens next? Your business transforms into a powerhouse of high growth! Why? Because each team member starts thinking like an entrepreneur, constantly driven by the question: "How can I elevate our game and make things better, faster, and more efficient?" This fiery passion for progress ignites a wildfire of success, propelling your company to soar to new heights. Embrace this spirit of innovation, and watch your business become an unstoppable force of positive change.

Entrepreneurship and Innovation

At the end of the day, if your team members are thinking and behaving entrepreneurially, then they are going to be a lot more innovative. They will be able to think outside the box and transform both what you deliver and how you deliver it to your customers. They will find new solutions to old problems. They will be able to take calculated risks—and that should be encouraged.

Why is it better to be an innovative company? As an outcome of innovation, you see new technologies and processes being developed. You see people developing their own skills and talents. You see growth in areas that have been stagnant. As your innovation goes up, so does the value created for your customers and your employee experience. That means your company will grow faster than your competitors.

With the pace and competition of business today, if you do not have an entrepreneurial company, you will struggle with success. Entrepreneurship is, ultimately, all about value creation. It is about the courage and confidence to take risks. It is about taking ownership of your responsibilities, actions, and results.

And it means looking at the bigger picture. It is value- and results-driven, and when you start from a place of value creation—taking every asset and asking how every investment can produce better outcomes—it will significantly improve your ROI outcomes. The gains might be small at first, but as you empower your people to think like entrepreneurs, the needle will start to move, and the culture will gain momentum—as will your company's performance.

So, once you have the right talent, your team is aligned with your vision, and you have given them educational opportunities to help them think like entrepreneurs, what's next? In the following chapter, we will look at what happens when all the pieces are in place and how to continue to grow that success.

8

Employee Experience Blueprint – Cultivating Engagement, Productivity, and Retention

In today's fast-paced and remote work environment, cultivating an engaged and motivated workforce has become a top priority for organizations. However, many companies struggle with disengaged employees, experiencing issues like "quiet quitting" and bare minimum Mondays. There is a need for companies to redesign employee experience strategies built for the new talent landscape to achieve best-in-class employee engagement, productivity, and retention. By implementing this blueprint, you can unlock the true potential of your workforce and yield remarkable results, with business growth reaching 11x levels.

Employee Experience Strategies

By incorporating these strategies into your organization's practice and design, you can ensure that your employees are engaged, that their needs are met, that areas of growth are actively addressed, and that you can achieve a truly transformational way of relating to each other.

Rethink Employee Journey: Nurturing engagement from applicant to exit in the new workplace. Many companies have well-put-together customer experience journeys, but they don't have an employee experience journey. Understand crucial stages for the employee journey, such as applicant and candidate experience, onboarding process, performance management, growth opportunities, and even the exit experience.

Factors Influencing Employee Engagement: It is important to understand and manage what impacts employee engagement, including aspects like health and well-being, family support, competitive compensation and benefits, recognition and rewards, company culture, and effective leadership.

Employee Priorities: Understand what truly matters to employees in your organization, encompassing meaningful work, supportive leaders, psychological safety, a positive work environment, growth opportunities, and recognition for their contributions to have an effective engagement plan.

Engagement Drivers: Uncover the drivers that ignite and sustain employee engagement, such as a strong brand reputation, a people-centric and collaborative culture, a nurturing learning environment, abundant career opportunities, clear role, and goal clarity, a mature performance system, consistent recognition, supportive HR policies, work-life balance initiatives, and a genuine commitment to valuing employees.

Great Engagement Requires Complete Care, Connection, and Collaboration

"Sunny, how do you keep your employees engaged, drive loyalty and build a healthy work community culture at IT By Design?"

That's a common question I get from my fellow business leaders and entrepreneurs. Like many business owners, I have tried several different ways to engage team members because it's such a vital piece of an overall culture (talent) strategy. Some of the ways I tried didn't work; some proved only mildly successful. I want to share a program that has produced the best results so far during my Talentpreneurial journey.

We developed a framework called Life By Design (LBD) for complete employee care and connection. It is a transformational employee engagement program that goes way beyond traditional engagement practices. We encourage our employees as they first create their life plans, and then we provide opportunities to support them using the LBD framework. It takes care of four important pillars of their life—health, relationships, career, and legacy.

Life By Design, NOT By Default

Fostering genuine engagement and a feeling of belonging at work requires holistic employee care, connection, and collaboration. My journey to living a Life By Design started with learning from my business peer groups. Most of the peer forums help you develop a personal and professional life plan. As a member of the Young President Organization (YPO) and other business peer groups such as Evolve (formerly known as HTG), I have learned to create and maintain my own life plan.

In 2020, during the COVID lockdown, I was challenged with keeping my team safe and protecting their confidence and well-being when they started working from home. There were a lot of security and safety challenges, especially for our India staff. I used my peer group learnings to develop the "Life By Design" framework for my employees.

In March 2020, I started a daily morning Zoom call called "Coffee with Community," which was a virtual hour-long session. Building this platform for my employee voice was my way of being there for the team during scary times. Our daily agenda was "Ask me anything." Then we would proceed to chat about how they and their family were doing and how we could help. It evolved every week with additional items, including surveys and polls based on the "employee voice" rooted in this simple question. A lot of employees wanted us to support them with security, safety, and mental wellness, so we hired a yoga and meditation coach from the birthplace of Yoga (Rishikesh, India) for daily wellness sessions. In our India office, using my network, I brought in local law enforcement leaders (e.g., police chief equivalent contacts) who addressed their local safety issues (access to basic needs such as food, medicine, etc. issues during lockdown) to make sure that everyone felt safe and secure. Based on the needs and feedback of our work community, we enhanced the benefits plan and offered a few additional engagement activities such as dance classes, a book club, fitness and wellness, virtual happy hours, and an internal hotline for emergency purposes.

The employees formed a volunteer Culture Committee that started a Go-Givers program to help the internal IT By Design employees. They then expanded the program to help local communities get access to food, medicine, oxygen concentrators, blankets, and clothing. The team personally donated to the company fund to expand the impact of these committees. These programs kept evolving thanks to the commitment of the Culture Team of volunteers to continuous transformation.

In 2022, Life By Design started gaining more momentum and eventually evolved to a life planning process for all employees. We hired professionals to design a complete employee care program and added it to our employee review process. Everyone at IT By Design is encouraged and supported to live Life By Design, NOT By Default.

By focusing on four key areas of planning and goal setting—life wheels: Health, Relationships, Career, and Legacy—we aim to create a thriving community where employees can truly unlock the full potential of their lives.

The four areas are:

- *Health By Design* – We focus on healthy habits and mindsets for fitness, nutrition, and mental and spiritual wellness. We bring thought leaders to educate and provide guidance and support for employees to do well in these areas.

- *Relationships By Design* – We focus on educating people about healthy relationships (spouse, children, friends, etc.) as well as social life (recreational activities, bucket list, etc.). We cover topics such as the impact of toxic relationships and what best practices are to build and maintain healthy relationships. This emphasizes the value of surrounding yourself with positive and growth mindset people.

- *Career By Design* – This area aims to place a focus on how we can support employees in planning their career roadmap, financial life (money and retirement), and intellectual life (education and learning). We help them develop learning and growth paths to keep their momentum going.

• *Legacy By Design* – We support and empower employees to give back, succeed in succession planning, and engage in service life (community activities, etc.). Everyone is empowered and encouraged to participate in Go-Givers activities with time, talent, and treasure.

I'll refer to these four categories as the "Four Wheels of Life," and if you can keep them in harmony as you would the tires on your car for better mileage and a smoother ride, your life can run very smoothly, too.

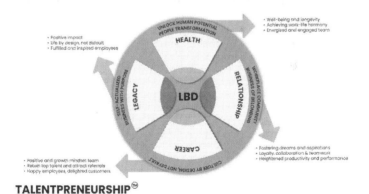

LBD®| LIFE BY DESIGN

TALENTPRENEURSHIP™

The Program Structure

As part of the way Life By Design is set up, each week, I will personally invite a health professional, life coach, or other subject matter expert (SME) to a weekly Zoom session where they share their best practices with the employees who attend. I even open the sessions to employees' family members. Each week we focus on a different aspect of our lives. For instance, a world-class sleep doctor presented a session on sleep health disciplines and resources; a cardiologist presented helpful information about heart health that we can all easily apply; a nutritionist helped with healthy eating plans; and a fitness instructor with an exercise routine. I have brought in mental wellness, sleep, heart, career, finance, and legacy experts. Each presentation lasts approximately 45 minutes and is followed by a 15-minute Q&A.

On alternate weeks, I conduct my own presentations, during which I use the time to support the team with their plan updates, reflect on their progress, and celebrate their personal and professional wins. I share what I learn, my experiences, my habits from exercise and nutrition, and the ways I'm improving my life in the four key areas. We'll also reflect on the lessons we learned from previous presenters, share how we're implementing those lessons in our daily lives, and highlight the benefits that we're realizing.

The intent of LBD is to build a happy and healthy community at IT By Design by promoting healthy habits and mindsets and providing development tools and resources that extend far beyond traditional employee care programs. Its outcomes are tremendous:

- Employees can reflect on their personal and professional vision of success.

- They learn practical ways to maintain their well-being and that of their families.
- Personal challenges can be addressed during sessions or through private communication.
- Improved happiness and health lead to happy customers and increased productivity for the business.
- A genuine commitment to employee well-being builds a strong sense of community and mutual growth.

The Life By Design program also gives my IT By Design managers great insight into their employees' needs and wants, so now they are aware of their team's personal and professional visions of success. Armed with that important information, our leaders can now help their respective employees achieve those goals—making for even happier and more productive individuals and teams.

Implementing Life by Design

One of the great upsides to Life By Design is that it doesn't cost a lot of time or funds to introduce it into your talent strategy. I have brought most of the experts from my business peer groups based on the relationships, and it only costs a thank you email and willingness to barter time, talent, and treasure. Entrepreneurs normally have a wealthy network, and they just need to be intentional to serve their team. While we do have some paid expert engagements such as life, fitness, yoga, and meditation coaches, it is the best investment that we are making in our people that builds a healthy business and lives in the business.

Assign a program manager, such as your key leaders, HR, or office admin, and provide direction. This is important because for this type of program to succeed, it must have executive team sponsorship. Build a culture team of volunteers (culture ambassadors). Support the program manager and culture team by creating a program charter and a list of potential guest speakers based on employee needs and wants that you have identified during surveys and other employee voice/feedback systems. You probably already have a lot of experts in your network (e.g., specialists in your business or social circles). Your program manager can plan and coordinate virtual sessions based on your set rhythm and run the logistics of the event just like your other company events.

You can regularly conduct online surveys with team participants and ask what areas they would like to see your program cover. This gives your culture direction to bring relevant and relatable content. Get your team excited about it and emphasize the benefits they can experience from participating. Initially, attendance may be light, but if done right, the attendees will share their enthusiasm for it, and you'll see attendance numbers grow.

If nothing else, a Life By Design (LBD) program will demonstrate to your entire community your genuine desire to help them enhance their personal and professional lives. It can strengthen your culture and build a healthy community at work. A culture of community attracts other people with similar mindsets and values—your healthy work community grows organically.

Transformational Employee Care Program: A complete employee care program should go beyond compensation and benefits, like the LBD framework mentioned above. We support our employees in designing their life plans using the LBD framework. This program had a huge impact on our employee experience program and has strengthened our culture. As you can see in the following graphic, we consider our employees' holistic, long-term life plans as well, including those key considerations of health, relationships, career, and legacy, in the immediate future as well as the more distant future.

LIFE BY DESIGN PLAN™

Wheels of Life	Today	5 Years	10 Years	15 Years	20 Years
#HealthByDesign					
Physical Life					
Mental Life					
Spiritual Life					
#RelationshipsByDesign					
Family Life					
Friends Life					
Social Life					
#CareerByDesign					
Work Life					
Financial Life					
Intellectual Life					
#LegacyByDesign					
Service Life					
Legacy Life					
Succession Life					

Great Engagement Requires Great Communication

To build a strong bond with your team members, communication is the magical key. Let them see the clear vision you hold for the company's future, and keep them in the loop about every thrilling development along the way. Nurture that shared understanding of the grand mission and the journey we're on together. As a leader, your own clarity is the fuel that ignites the passion in others. Know your vision like the back of your hand and express it in a way that fuels your personal ambition. Embrace the dialogue with yourself, seeking those profound goals that drive your every step.

You must also give your team—and the wider community—the opportunity to communicate with you about their concerns, needs, and desires. You need their buy-in if you want to succeed. Without communication, there is no alignment.

You can use a multitude of approaches and platforms, which we will discuss in this chapter. At IT By Design, we use a mix of monthly state of the company or town hall meetings; question and answer sessions; Friday weekly email recaps; newsletters; and morning huddles via Zoom or other video chat software. Your goal is cohesive and comprehensive communication over multiple platforms, facilitating a two-way street. Each of these is an essential tool in your toolbox for communicating meaningfully with your team. As Ramsey Sahyoun says, "Our culture is very entrepreneurial. Our top core value is empowerment, and we believe that people do their best work when they are empowered to drive outcomes instead of just being dictated to. When people know what is happening, they feel connected, and then they are more productive and more engaged."

But if communication is so important, why do so few companies do it effectively—or at all? Why is it so rare?

Your Opportunity in Communication

Before we get into solutions, we first need to understand the problems. Lack of communication or ineffectual communication is a major factor when it comes to low-performing companies and low productivity among staff. The challenge is even greater in the post-COVID world because so many people now work remotely or on a hybrid home/office schedule. People are not in one place to be able to communicate regularly and create that sense of teamwork. Technology like Microsoft Teams and Zoom do help address this to a degree, but the extent to which a company utilizes these tools and to what effect is at the heart of the issue. If a company—and more so if the leaders of a company—does not prioritize communication, it can negatively affect their relationship with their team and the employee's relationships with one another.

It can be easy to let things slide. Companies are essentially people, and people, especially people in leadership positions, are busy. We are so busy! Our calendars are always full of meetings, conferences, strategic reviews, planning sessions—you name it. It can seem as though there aren't enough hours in the day. Sometimes, it feels like the business is running *you* rather than the other way around. We all, at times, fall victim to the "tyranny of the urgent." There are fires to put out and urgent matters to address. Getting everyone together for a motivational session on vision and community can seem not only pointless but impossible.

We all have different challenges and priorities when it comes to the "why" of not communicating. But you have to make time for your people. You need to be intentional when it comes to communication. Put strategies in place and build the discipline of communication.

Another solution to the problem of being too busy to communicate is to limit the number of direct reports you have. It is common to see executive leadership, especially CEOs and the like, take on too much. Rather than focusing on high-payoff activities, they often overload themselves with an abundance of smaller but time-consuming low-payoff activities. A general rule of best practice is that a CEO or senior leadership member should only manage five to seven people, at most, if you want to optimize your own time. Any more than that, and your efficiency is going to plummet. You will spend too much time managing and directing other people's work rather than having time to focus on your own work of generating and implementing ideas for growing your company. Time is a valuable resource. If you are always chasing your tail, you will not have time to communicate regularly and effectively with your team, especially in the wider reaches of your company.

To do this, you need to think about structure. What structure is going to benefit your company most? A solid structure will focus on what needs to be done to achieve success, creating roles that align with that vision and then filling those roles based on your people's strengths. It also begs the question, what is your leadership style? To be an effective leader, you need to be able to recruit and train a team you trust so that they can, in turn, take the reins on their own projects and lead their own teams. If you are growth oriented and you want to be able to scale your business, the only way to achieve that is by having a good team with you on the journey. That is a lot easier to fulfill if you know everyone is aligned with your mission and values.

Part of the origin of this problem lies in the fact that many CEOs and executives, especially in the tech field, are what I would call "accidental entrepreneurs." A lot of tech CEOs got their start, well, in tech. For many, their backgrounds are in computer science, software engineering, or information technology rather than business. They founded a start-up that grew into a major player in the space. But their instincts are basically still those of tech people or engineers. They have not made the shift to an entrepreneurial mindset. (Another reason why lifelong learning is so important!)

Not every accidental entrepreneur is a "people person" either, but learning soft skills, management tools, and leadership techniques are just as essential to success—to keeping your team engaged and productive—as having the best platform or software on the market. Again, people are your best asset. For example, you can make hard business decisions, and you can *also* be kind in how you communicate those decisions. Learn how to communicate the respect and dignity you and your company have for other human beings while making those hard decisions for your business. It will serve you in the long run!

The return on investment is really limitless if it means keeping your top talent. As we have discussed, the ROI on good communication is employee retention—top talent retention. Retaining your top talent means retaining your top customers. Remember, employee churn and customer churn are highly interconnected. Better employee retention also means, from an ROI perspective, lower cost per hire and lower cost per employee over annualized cost because there are a lot of costs involved if you have to back-fill a position, so employee retention reduces those costs. The bottom line is that communication is essential if you are going to keep your team happy, engaged, and productive.

Our Business Is to Be HAPPY

So, what does good communication look like? At IT By Design, we have a multi-pronged approach to ensure we are communicating with our team at every level, efficiently, effectively, and often. Let's begin with a look at the monthly state of the company meetings. On the first Monday of the month, we hold a company-wide meeting. Just one hour out of every month. Our purpose in holding these meetings is to build a strong community among the three pillars of IT By Design. That includes our staff colleagues, our customer partners or MSP partners, and our strategic partners or solution partners (such as other tech companies like Cisco, which support the community through thought leadership, among other things). Altogether, we have about six hundred people in attendance at our monthly State of the Company meetings, so they are critical for big-picture ideas, bolstering motivation, and keeping everyone on the same page moving forward. And, even though each pillar has its own role to fulfill in the business, we are ultimately one community working together toward common goals. It is all about the people—people, people, people! We want people to feel connected, support each other, and facilitate positive mindsets.

According to Jack Daly,

> There are four cornerstones when building culture. One is recognition systems. People are dying for recognition. Recognize your people in so many different ways, and it doesn't have to be financial. Second is communication systems. Third is personal and professional development processes. The fourth is empowerment processes, which is creating an environment where people are enabled or

encouraged to make decisions as if they were the owner—as opposed to seeking approval from the boss.

To foster that sense of community support and positive mindset, we always look at our values during the state of the company meetings. We use an acronym for our community values, which we call HAPPY community. "H" stands for humility; "A" for accountability; "P" for positivity; "P" for passion; and "Y" for your community. To dig a little further, here is what we mean by each of these values. Humility is the ability to listen generously and the motivation to learn and grow yourself and your team. Accountability means speaking clearly and honestly and honoring your commitments. Positivity is just that: we want people to maintain a positive focus and to appreciate and acknowledge their community; we emphasize gains, not gaps. The second "P" for passion is all about knowing your passions and strengths and positioning yourself well to align with the greater good and company vision. And last but certainly not least is "Your community," which means being there for each other in the good times and the bad.

After that, I review the state of the company. What's our focus? How did we do last month? What's our focus for the next month? Then we dive into the next layer, and each department head will give an update on what's happening in their department and how that impacts other departments and the company as a whole. We call this cross-functional communication.

Then, we celebrate the wins. This is really essential. It is important to show appreciation for people if you want to build alignment and engagement. So, for example, if we receive positive feedback about an employee from a customer or praise from a manager, I will highlight that.

We also give team members an opportunity to share an appreciation for one another, and this really emphasizes teamwork and community values on a personal level. We talk about events that are coming up in the company that people need to know about, including some of the health sessions and team-building events we discussed in the previous chapter. We also do a question-and-answer session at the end. It is very conversational and candid. People love the connection and the clarity they get from these meetings. They *want* to know what's happening in the company. There is a common expression in business that, "The employee knows how, but the boss knows why." Sharing the "why" of it all will make your employees feel more empowered and, therefore, more invested.

It is so vital to cultivate a culture of collaboration and teamwork because that is what drives a community committed to continuous transformation. I want a company and community that is dedicated to lifelong learning and development—that is what I count as a win. We want to nurture a focus on positive and growth mindsets. A rising tide lifts all boats is the ethos at the heart of our community. These are the values and mindsets and vision that will bring your people together. And if people feel they are embedded in a community, that leads to higher engagement and retention. After all, you want to keep your talent—and that means keeping them happy and engaged.

Small Talk, Big Impact

It is not enough to do the big-picture sessions once a month. If you want to continuously cultivate engagement, you need to communicate clearly and often. Any opportunity you have to make a connection with your team—through chat, email, Zoom, or in person—is an opportunity to reinvigorate and realign them with your core values and vision. But you also need to keep in mind that your time—and your employees' time—is a valuable resource. So, what can you do to communicate that will have the biggest impact without taking out an equally big chunk of time from your schedule?

One of the most effective communication tools I use is a weekly email. Every Friday, I send a weekly recap to the whole staff. It is a short email that highlights different things going on in the company. A lot of it is my own thoughts: where I think everyone can contribute, what is the focus for the week, where should we as a company be directing our attention? And I always include a section on what I am proud of when it comes to my team. I want it to be informational but also inspirational. I also include anything that was recorded recently—seminars, health sessions, the state of the company (if the email is at the start of the month). It is yet another effective way to provide information and clarity to your staff. Think about it in terms of communication with a customer. With any customer, you want to achieve a certain number of touchpoints because those touchpoints lead to increased engagement and more business. It is the same with your employees.

We have also introduced morning huddles, a practice that is very common in corporate America, mainly because it is so effective. A morning huddle is a short, focused session—usually just fifteen minutes—conducted within your small team. For instance, I do my daily huddle with my next layer of direct reports. We always start the session by discussing a win from the day before. That sets the tone for the day and gets everyone on a positive footing. Then we can quickly discuss if anyone on the team is stuck and make a plan for getting them the support they need that day. We finish by going over what each person's focus and goals are for the day. What do you need to do to achieve your crucial result for the day? Morning huddles use a layered approach. So, from my huddle, my direct reports will then have another short session with their team, and so on, down the line.

As we have discussed, good communication goes both ways. To that end, we also use a Net Promoter Score (NPS) for employees on a quarterly basis. An NPS is a benchmark to measure customer loyalty, satisfaction, and enthusiasm for a company. We want to know, would you recommend us to your peers? Would you recommend us to your friends? We want to know how they feel about the company, the work they do, and the support they receive. We are looking to gauge employee sentiment, so we know what's working and what we might change to improve employee satisfaction and experience. We also use customer satisfaction (C-SAT) surveys on a monthly basis and Team GPS, which provides us with feedback and enables employees to engage with their peers. With these surveys, you can drill down a little further for answers to more specific questions. We ask things like are you happy with your benefits, or are you happy with your manager? And it is important to note that these surveys are all anonymous. In order for them to work, people need to feel they can be honest.

Tools like this are extremely useful for providing perspective on your company culture. We have gained a lot of new insights from the data collected. For example, as a result of our C-SAT surveys, we realized that our employees in the US were unhappy with their benefits package. I thought our health benefits were very strong in the US. Then I realized from the survey that, actually, the US teams wanted us to review their healthcare benefits. We took immediate action. That is the whole idea of any survey, you have to take action. You cannot respond to every actionable item, but you can and should take action on the top three to five things. Take action, make an impact, and then report back to the team.

The result of these lines of communication is cultural transformation. Thanks to good communication, our people are more aligned with our goals; we have seen increased results at the top and bottom lines, and it has had a huge impact in terms of everyone's contribution because people know where and how they can contribute effectively to the company.

The Elements of Good Communication

Not all communication is created equal. How many times has someone joked, "That meeting could have been an email"? All too often, it was no joke. The meeting *should* have been an email. Good communication needs to be meaningful, focused, and consistent. Always start with a purpose. Your daily communication is going to differ from your weekly or monthly communication. Daily communication should focus more on everyday details. What is on your team's workflow for the day? If a team member is stuck on a particular task, are you able to help them?

Whether you realize it or not, there is a kind of communication happening when you take the time to support your team. On a weekly basis, you can start to broaden the scope to include communicating bigger-picture things like your overall vision, weekly numbers, and short-term goals. You and your team need to communicate what's working and what's not working and take a hard look at your most important numbers. This is the time to determine the main issues affecting your team and brainstorm solutions that you can put in place to address them. Then, you can implement those practices in order to hit your numbers or other business plan objectives.

Lastly, on a monthly basis, you can review the previous month's successes and pain points, and you can start planning and adjusting for the next month. Quarterly meetings should focus on a deeper analysis of the preceding three months and realigning your projections for the following quarter. The same goes for annual reviews. You want a really deep dive into your numbers and objectives and how they fit with the big picture. At all times, you want to communicate purpose, vision, and core values.

Good communication happens at every level. So, not only do we have the big all-community meetings, but it is also just as important to have communication at every level of your organization. Each department should be mirroring these lines of communication because, ultimately, you want alignment at every level. Remember, the reward for good communication is alignment. Think of it this way: you're resetting every month, in terms of attention and focus, so that you can change things that need to be changed and produce the best outcome for your company and your people.

Cultivate Your Garden

The right team members, if they are aligned with your vision and your value system, will be bolstered and reinvigorated by these meetings. We get really positive feedback from people afterward. Mission and vision alignment is a great way to figure out who your "right people" are. At my company, we have experienced people who, when they join us, think they have the right mindsets and alignment with the vision. And, of course, we think so, too—that's why we hired them!

Generally, within the first ninety days, you get to know people really well through all this communication and engagement. And sometimes we, or they, discover that the way we function and work is not for them. Not everyone is going to be the right fit—and that's okay. What is not okay is keeping those people employed. It can be hard to let people go, especially when so much of the drive behind all this communication and engagement is the goal of retention. I know what it costs to lose talent. But an essential lesson in any business is learning to let go of that which does not serve you.

What that means, in the long run, is that for those people who stay with us six months and beyond, those people are 100% committed to our community and aligned with our values. The proof is in the pudding. If you visit LinkedIn or similar professional sites, you will find a number of testimonials and videos from IT By Design. I do a career corner conversation every week. I pick one person from the team to interview, and we discuss how they feel about the company, the culture, their work—everything. People genuinely feel like one big family, and we treat each other as such, with dignity and respect. I can talk to a building services staff in any of our offices—in India, the Philippines, or the US—and they feel the same kinship with us because I show them the same respect that I show everyone.

Although it's easy to focus solely on numbers and performance objectives, the beauty of this business model lies in the immense personal rewards it offers. It brings joy and fulfillment on a profound level. When I look at it through the lens of Maslow's Hierarchy of Needs, I experience a sense of self-actualization. I am living my life's purpose, my dream life. I can tangibly feel the positive impact I, my company, and those around me are making. It goes beyond mere profit-making and business management; it's about making a global impact. By providing jobs, purpose, and a thriving community centered on respect and human dignity, I am fulfilling a meaningful need. This purpose-driven approach gives me a profound sense of fulfillment and a greater purpose to serve. It's not just about financial success; it's about contributing to something much larger than myself and finding true meaning in every step of this journey.

Don't get me wrong—money is important if you want to have a sustainable business. Financial stability will help protect your entire community, so your profit and loss statement needs to be healthy, but that is not my primary driver. We are now a fifteen-million-dollar business, and if those many million didn't satisfy me, then another million, another ten million is not going to satisfy me either. No, my primary driver is to build a community of people working toward the same vision, and those people help take care of the institution. They take care of the company. Money gives you options and resources to serve others, and greater success puts you in a position to serve more and more people. This ethos and practice have served me well. The point is that you can have both: you can be successful *and* build a great community that supports people at every level. Great communication fosters higher engagement and longer retention and creates a happier, more connected workforce.

Communication is a key element of success and winning the talent war, but there is no one-size-fits-all solution. In the next chapter, we will look at what you need to do to meet the expectations and needs of the younger generations in the workforce. What do Millennials and Gen Zers need to feel happy and engaged at work?

9

The MrBeast Factor – What Millennials and Gen Zs Really Need

A s I write this book, I have three boys (of course, I am done) who are 21, 18, and 13 years of age, respectively. They are all Gen Zers—kids born between 1995 and 2012 (Millennials were born between 1981 and 1996.). Both of these populations constitute a significant portion of the workforce, especially in the tech sector. My kids asked a lot more "Why'" and "World Impact" questions in the first ten years of their lives than what I have asked in my entire life so far.

Gen Z is the first generation to grow up fully immersed in a digital world. They are digital dragons (or doctors) with digital dementia from birth. They have an inherent need for constant digital connectivity, which means they rely heavily on smartphones, social media, and instant communication platforms to stay connected with peers, access information, and express themselves. They place a significant emphasis on social and environmental issues. In fact, I got to know about MrBeast, his clean-up crews, and robots that clean the sea from my 13-year-old. My two oldest boys (both in college) are passionate about causes like climate change, social justice, and equality. Having grown up in an era of global interconnectedness, they seek purpose-driven careers and companies that align with their values.

My Gen Z team members at IT By Design prioritize emotional well-being and seek environments that support mental health, flexible work arrangements, and stress-reducing activities. I have noticed that Gen Zers make up the highest number of attendees at our "Life By Design" sessions on mental health and well-being.

Despite all this, hardly a day goes by without a headline about the disengagement or "quiet quitting" of Millennials and Gen Zs. In this chapter, we will explain how to meet the expectations of younger team members. They need more frequent conversations than older workers. They need clarity—no gray areas! We will explore connecting with them via social media, like using TikTok instead of Facebook and Microsoft Teams instead of email.

It may seem like a shift in the wrong direction, but these changes can help your company utilize new technology more effectively and inject new energy into your workplace community. Above all, Millennials and Zoomers want to make an impact in the world. That means they are eager to fulfill a mission and vision—and that is a good thing. Ramsey Sahyoun put it: "I think people in any generation want clear expectations as to what success in their role looks like. They also want to be empowered at work and to feel like their opinions are valued. They also want to be inspired by the mission of the company they work for and feel like what they do is impactful. So it's incumbent upon us as leaders to deliver on those things." Their main question is: how will my work make the world a better place? So, how can you meet their needs and get them aligned with your company's goals and values? In other words, how can you develop Millennials and Zoomers into top talent?

Teenage Wasteland

Millennials came of age during the era of 9/11 and the war on terror, the Global Financial Crisis and subsequent Great Recession, and the rise of the internet age. They had a harder time finding entry-level jobs after college, lived at home with their parents longer than the previous generation, and had a more difficult time getting on the property ladder.

Gen Z arrived on their heels. They are the first generation for whom a smartphone was their first phone (and have likely never seen a rotary or corded phone!) and have grown up immersed in the world of social media. For many, their first president was Barack Obama, and the idea of a black president was a foregone conclusion instead of a long-dreamed-of, hard-won goal. Not only are they the largest generation, but they are also the most racially and ethnically diverse in the US. Although Gen Z was set to walk into the professional world at a time when the economy was strong, and there was record-low unemployment, COVID-19 changed all that.

And, while some of us may still think of Millennials and Zoomers as "just kids," they are now all adults (elder Millennials, in fact, are over forty) and are part of every workplace. Their presence has brought along with it a shift in attitude, expectations, and cultural norms. Gone are the days of finding a steady job and building a lifelong career at

SUNNY KAILA

one company. They are not there for the "grind" and tend to focus more on "work to live" rather than "live to work."

Though Millennials and Zoomers have their differences, what both have in common is that they want their work to be meaningful; they want to change the world. They want to know how their work is going to make an impact and leave the world a better place. They have greater access to information, and they have been raised to think globally. They are more concerned with broad issues like climate change and social justice. According to a study by McKinsey & Company, "Gen Zers value individual expression and avoid labels. They mobilize themselves for a variety of causes."[14] In contrast, Millennials are more idealistic and more confrontational.[15]

Again, they are both products of the digital age. Millennials are attached to their devices. Gen Zers are the most internet-dependent generation and are at the forefront of technology use.[16] "This generation thinks and acts very differently. Their connectedness, their ability to navigate change quickly, and their desire to have a positive impact on the world are all reflected in their higher expectations of technology and organizations," says Jason Dorsey, president of The Center for Generational Kinetics, which conducted the study.

Millennials and Zoomers also have a different attitude towards capitalism, generally—perhaps as a result of growing up during the Great Recession or post-recession. Theirs are the generations that backed Bernie Sanders, universal healthcare, and the Green New Deal. We have a lot of employees based in India and the Philippines, and we increasingly hear that if they are moving to the West for jobs or education, it is to Canada more so than the US because of the social welfare networks there.

120

The notion of risk-reward, of working hard, of earning your way through a career is changing. Instead, they want flexibility—flexible hours, flex days, and unlimited vacation time. They seek emotional fulfillment from their work as much as they want the paycheck (or direct debit, as it were). It would be easy to call this new mentality "entitlement," and in some ways, it is, but instead of looking at their attitudes with disdain, as many in the older generations tend to do, it is important to appreciate that it is more complex. This difference in worldview and lack of understanding can lead to a divide among your team members.

What We Have Here Is a Failure to Communicate

So, what happens if you fail to recognize the unique mindset and needs of younger workers? What are the downsides going to be? The research is clear, as one study notes, "Without proper understanding of this generation, organizations will find difficulties to hire and retain them for the sustainable growth of the organizations. By understanding them, companies can determine what can impact their recruitment and retention success through paying attention to what makes this generation tick in the workplace."[17]

If you fail to work well with Millennials and Zoomers, the biggest issues for your company are going to be a lack of alignment and employee churn. A lack of alignment means low productivity and employee churn means higher costs to you and a decline in the customer experience. The fact of the matter is that these are the people who are replacing the retiring older workforce. They are tech savvy, having grown up in the internet and social media eras, and they do have a lot to offer—if you know how to retain and motivate them. Arlin Sorensen says that successful companies are not filled with clones of their entrepreneurial owners but smart and motivated teams that evaluate every idea and create work groups that identify and execute the best. He adds, "My companies began to grow when I got over hiring people who thought and acted like me (the easy button) and hired people with the right character, skill, and desire to help our companies succeed. It's not about sitting around the campfire singing songs together but having perspective and analysis from every side of the opportunities and challenges we face. Only then will you maximize the success of your organization."

Like so many problems in life, the first port of call for finding a solution is communication. There is a need for a conversation, a meeting of minds between these two perspectives in order to reconcile them. That conversation needs to center on the reality that there is no substitute for hard work. If you want to change the world for the better, but you don't want to get out of bed, that is not going to work. You might have the best of intentions and aspirations, but you have to pay the dues to affect that change.

I like to call this the "MrBeast Factor." If you do not know MrBeast, he is a hugely successful YouTuber who began posting videos when he was just thirteen years old. He has over 130 million subscribers, an estimated personal net worth of $106 million, and his business has been valued at $1.5 billion.[18] He landed the number one spot on *Forbes'* Top Creators of 2022 and Highest-Paid YouTube Stars of 2022.[19] He is only twenty-four years old. He is also a big philanthropist, and a major part of his platform is giving back and changing the world.

Among his followers and subscribers, there is an impression of this high-flying, easy lifestyle where he is making money hand-over-fist simply for sitting at a computer a couple of hours a day and uploading content. The reality could not be further from the truth. He has a vision of the impact he wants to make, and he works incredibly hard to achieve it. He has discipline and business acumen, and he is extremely talented at what he does. He has the grit to make it happen.

So, the first step in addressing this disconnect is listening to your younger team members and understanding where they are coming from. Find out what their aspirations are. This is also supported by the literature, which finds they want "managers to listen to their ideas and value their opinions."[20]

We are all familiar with Dan Sullivan's D.O.S. tool— eliminate your biggest danger, capture your biggest opportunity, and maximize your biggest strength. Both sides of this conversation have dangers, opportunities, and strengths, and it's important to recognize and acknowledge that. Each generation has its own strengths and weaknesses. From there, you can figure out how to create greater value together and a better future that you would not be able to create alone.

The Kids Are All Right

Millennials and Zoomers have different mentalities, but they also have a different skill set, a skillset that can be leveraged to the advantage of their team members and your company's performance. Older workers have one set of abilities, and younger workers have another. So, if we can even think of the Strategic Coach perspective of combining capabilities, then you can create a very unique value. If you fail to understand and embrace their talents, you will lose out on a valuable opportunity.

Younger workers are tuned into social media in a way older workers generally are not. They post more, engage more, and more of their mental well-being and confidence is linked to likes and retweets. It has been well established that social media users get a dopamine hit in response to positive feedback online or even just from scrolling through their phones. Their brains are wired to the speed of the internet.

Business technology reflects that mentality. Now, instead of email as the primary mode of business communication, Microsoft Teams and Zoom messaging and video calls have become the norm. This also means that Millennials and Zoomers have a level of tech fluency that older workers may lack. They can pick up new technology quicker and identify new applications or areas of development ahead of the curve. On top of that, they are used to the speed of communication, having been raised in the digital age. If you want something done quickly, these are the people you want doing it. They can be aces when it comes to rapid, efficient customer service and experience.

And because of the "failure to launch" syndrome early in their careers—in part caused by the Great Recession and other financial pressures as much as shifting attitudes—younger workers, especially Millennials, are keen for a sense of independence. If you are able to clarify the goal, their role, and the expectations set for them, you can then give them the autonomy to achieve it.

At the macro level, when talking about expectations, focus on outcomes. They want to know, *What is the outcome that you want from me?* I suggest outlining the target, giving them the outcome, and then letting them come up with the options to achieve said outcome. Use your experience to guide and coach them. Offer strategies for success and be very clear and explicit when it comes to numbers and goals. Clarity of objective is key because, for this group, ambiguity often means anxiety.

Another important factor is to impart the "why" of objectives. Why do they need to do this? Why is it important? What is the meaning of the product? They need something more than a directive to go out and sell $200,000 worth of products and services. Again, this might seem like more work for you, your managers, and your leadership team, but these questions will actually help this cohort of employees become more invested in your goals and visions. If you can show them the big picture, they can help deliver it.

Everything Is Accelerating

There are some clear generational dividing lines. Do you use Facebook or Tik Tok®? Messenger or Snapchat®? Do you search for answers on Google®, or do you use ChatGPT? Do you take notes on your iPad® or with a pen and paper? Wherever you land—and more importantly, wherever your team members land—there are skills and strengths to be leveraged. The technology transformation is still ongoing, and the pace of progress is only accelerating. The baseline is shifting, and your company needs to move with the times if you do not want to be left in the past while your competitors advance into the future.

The best way to stay relevant and keep the new talent pool onside is by starting with the purpose of your company. You and your employees need a purpose bigger than yourself. In the next chapter, we will talk about how to design that purpose, build a happy, healthy workplace community, and align your team with your values to make an impact on the world.

10

The Result – Self-Managed and Profitable Business While Transforming Lives—Including Your Own

Now, you have a talent-centric mindset! You are a true Talentpreneur. It is no longer about you as the sole leader. Instead, you are building a true "community at work" while positively impacting your people. You care about people beyond their careers. You care about their growth. You understand your people, and you're positioning them to take advantage of their superpowers by clearly defining job roles and performance criteria. You are providing talent mapping, taking into account their strengths and point of view. You have an alignment of core values. As a result, you are winning the talent war and creating a great Culture By Design with the help of your Talentpreneur skills and TOS.

We have come a long way. We have talked about the tremendous pressures of attracting and retaining top talent in the post-pandemic world and the problem of quiet quitting in the middle of projects. We discussed how to assess the (sometimes conflicting) needs of your company and the desires of your employees when it comes to home and hybrid working. We've explored methods to enhance productivity and engagement, attract younger talent, nurture your teams' strengths, and foster effective communication strategies within your workplace community.

We've gone through the pain, the growth, and the solutions your business needs to win the talent war. You have all the tools to bring your company and your team to the forefront of success. So, what are the results you might expect once you start implementing "By Design" practices?

- **People Transformation:** You will witness your team members achieve their dreams and know you had a hand in their success. They will see your genuine concern for helping them live their lives to their fullest potential. That attitude will be reflected in the way they support your customers, improving your customer service and increasing your customer retention rate. Congratulations! You are now creating a culture by design, not by default.

- **Collaboration/Teamwork:** Those happier team members will give greater support to each other throughout your organization, increasing productivity, heightening innovation, and unlocking the potential for each of their cohorts. With this, their level of appreciation for each other will dramatically increase.

- **Continuous Business Transformation:** As I emphasized throughout this book, focus on your people first, and your business will grow exponentially. The transformation you will experience in your overall growth and profits will be astonishing. You will ask yourself, "Why didn't I do this sooner?"

Let's dive deeper into the results of implementing an effective TOS.

360-Degree Perspective

Success will vary from business to business, yet by adopting Talentpreneurship and employing the TOS along with Life By Design employee engagement framework outlined in earlier chapters, you can expect to achieve a profoundly productive team and workplace.

Beyond that, I hope you have changed a little in your own outlook and approach to your company and the team that supports you. Perhaps you are thinking more holistically about Life By Design and incorporating the four pillars, or "wheels of life," into your everyday operations and interaction. You are focused on your employees' health, relationships, career, and legacy—by design—and finding ways to support them in their goals. In other words, you are thinking and acting intentionally to achieve results.

I would like to take a moment to look back at the idea of 360-degree care of your employees, which is at the heart of my own outlook and business ethos and a driving force behind why I wanted to write this book. If you take the time and effort to listen to your employees and learn about their hopes, dreams, and aspirations, you will—without a doubt—see the results and reap the rewards. People want to be heard and valued. It is one of our most basic human needs to feel understood and to seek personal fulfillment and self-actualization. Incorporating these principles into your company's culture is a groundbreaking notion!

Put yourself in the shoes of your employees and imagine what it feels like to have you as an employer. Think about what it means to have your manager and your company thinking about you as a person and supporting you not only in your career growth but throughout every aspect of your life. Then think about how you would feel about your company knowing you so well. Picture the energy you would feel to help that company grow in the same way it has helped you grow. Making your employees feel seen will result in their desire to see the company succeed.

When people are invested in their work and aligned with your company's vision—your vision—you will find you have helped create a highly engaged team. Your employee experience will be the best in class, and your customer experience will be sterling standard because happy employees mean happy customers. When people are engaged, loyal, and committed, they project that to your customers.

Top Talent Retention

Another result we have seen at IT By Design since incorporating the TOS framework is that our top talent ratio has increased dramatically. From the people practices point of view, the most important number as a KPI for human resources is the percentage of employees at the company that are top talent. That is the best thing a business can have. If a high percentage of your company is made up of top talent *and* that top talent is fully engaged, that means widespread alignment—across every department and team—with your mission and vision.

This cohort is particularly driven and hungry to grow within the company. A high ratio of top talent increases the capacity for collaboration—and a little bit of healthy competition. When you are surrounded by people also striving to perform their best, it creates a circular feedback loop. What's more—thinking back to our discussion of helping people discover their superpowers and supporting their Career By Design goals—employees will have a clear path to grow their career with you, which means retention of top talent. They will be able to create a bigger future within the company using their career roadmap, which is the Career By Design aspect of Life By Design. Their interest in other positions at other workplaces will decrease. So, as a result of your high ratio of top talent, your employee retention across the board will go up, but especially your top talent retention.

Why is that *so* important? If we look at the bottom line, every employee who leaves costs you a lot of money. The expenses tied to hiring new staff are substantial. According to one recent study by the Society for Human Resource Management (SHRM)—an authority on benchmarks for human resources—employers spend on average nearly $5,000 on hiring and exponentially more for managerial roles.[21] Indeed, as the *Harvard Business Review* highlights, "Most of the $20 billion that companies spend on human resources vendors goes to hiring."[22]

That does not include staffing fees, onboarding, or training, nor does it include the cost of accretion. If you were to add that in, plus the cost of an unproductive first ninety-day provisional period—because let's be honest, if an employee is there and gone in three months, they have not contributed meaningfully or financially to your company or goals—then you also have to add in 25% of their salary to the cost per hire. Again, the SHRM study found that "Many employers estimate the total cost to hire a new employee can be three to four times the position's salary. That means if you're hiring for a job that pays $60,000, you may spend $180,000 or more to fill that role."[23]

The cost of onboarding new employees is guaranteed to affect your bottom line, especially if you have high employee churn. It will affect your profitability because employee churn always impacts and is directly associated with customer churn.

But we are done with the downsides now. Now, we have engagement and alignment from our top talent thanks to the community at work we have created. It is all about the quality of life you can provide for the people who are helping achieve your vision and mission.

More Than Numbers

When you transform the way people think about work, you transform everything they do. So, you might be running a software business, but when you leverage Life By Design, you are also making a tremendous positive impact on the people around you because you are not limiting your interaction with your people to Excel sheets and financials, which, sadly, is what a majority of businesses do.

Adapting to this change is crucial for your business, particularly as cultural norms evolve with the emergence of new generations. We're aware that Millennials and Zoomers are motivated by a strong inclination to be part of something larger than themselves and positively impact the world. By initiating a transformation within your workplace, you'll establish the very environment they aspire to create in order to make a meaningful global difference.

You will attract a lot of top talent and are more likely to retain it if you can appeal to younger workers and empower them to fulfill their sense of purpose. It may sound grandiose, but if what they want is to grow your business for you and make a positive impact, why not let them?

My point is this: people are your greatest asset. And people are more than numbers. Does that mean you have to ignore the numbers and the data when you create your people strategy? No, of course not. Those are important elements of your business strategy, too. But, when you see people for who they are, when you see them as a whole, you might *like* what you see in the numbers a whole lot more.

Customer Experience at Its Best

Have you ever walked into a café or restaurant and instantly knew that the person on the other side of the counter or standing by your table would rather be anywhere else in the world? You cannot hide an unhappy employee from a customer. Likewise, think of a time you interacted with someone who *loved* their job. Picture their enthusiasm and energy. That is something else you cannot hide from customers.

Employee experience and customer experience are like two peas in a pod—they go hand in hand. When you have engaged and aligned talent interacting with your customers, those customers will be getting the best service. They will want to keep growing your relationship. They will be inspired by the growth within your employees and your company, and they will want to grow with you.

Likewise, the relationship building between top customers and top talent is invaluable to your company. At the end of the day, your customers are also people, and the relationships they have with people in your company have value and meaning to them personally but also in the business-specific domains of reliability, partnership, and trust. When your customers are confident that their point of contact understands their approach, they will place their trust in you to cater to their needs. By retaining skilled employees and reducing turnover, your customers won't have to engage with new staff who are still in the learning process. Consequently, if your top-tier talent remains engaged, your key clients are likely to remain loyal as well.

Community at Work

What is the biggest impact of Talentpreneurship? When you build a great community at work—when you have shown through your actions that you care about your community members and their health, family, career, and legacy—that community will thrive.

Embrace professionalism and entrepreneurship to shape the life you desire. Through this transformation, not only will your own life improve, but you'll also empower others to follow suit. This journey will enrich your impact in your areas of influence, making it a truly beautiful experience.

If you use the tools that I have shared in this book, you will have a healthy workplace community. I can say, for my own part, my company has changed my life. I think back on my youth in a small village in India, to when I first came to the US as a teenager with such little experience of the world. I think of nights driving taxis in New York, of the precarious choice to further my education once I had paid off my debt, and about the early days of building the business. I could not have imagined so much was possible.

This company changed my life. My community at work has given me so much. I hope that I can give them the same. I want to uplift people. And I want *you* to experience this feeling, too. I want you to understand that when everyone shares one mission and one vision, everyone succeeds together. When you focus on culture, everything else falls into place.

And I want everyone who works to know this feeling. People *should* have the opportunity to feel purpose and fulfillment in their work—whatever it is they do. Whether they are sweeping the floors or designing your cloud technology, everyone deserves to feel valued and to be empowered to create value for others.

11

Should We Continue the Conversation?

We have come to the conclusion of the book, but perhaps not the conclusion of our conversation together. In addition to implementing the practices of Talentpreneurship at my own company, IT By Design is in the business of helping other companies, in particular Managed Service Providers (MSPs), with various aspects of growing their own businesses, building their talent strategies, and expediting their paths to self-managed and profitable business.

There are three primary services we provide that may be of interest to you. First, we offer a SaaS-based talent management system to help customers engage and retain talent and improve performance management. The second service we deliver is providing well-trained, world-class technical talent directly to give your company a leg up when it comes to winning the Talent Wars. We have ready-to-go talent to help build or expand your helpdesk. Additionally, the third service we provide is helping build your community at work by training your leaders and technicians and helping them develop their technical and leadership talents.

From the Strategic Coach perspective, our tools are like a talent triple play. If you are keen to grow your business and keep building your talent pool in line with your growth, here's a closer look at how IT By Design can help you achieve that goal.

Transform Your Talent with Team GPS

We have talked at length about the pressing need for 360-degree care of your talent to improve employee experience, boost productivity and engagement, and keep your top talent happy and aligned with your mission. Our SaaS-based talent transformation platform uses the 360-degree care model as the basis for developing a tailored talent strategy that works for you.

Our Team GPS tool is an all-in-one software solution to help improve employee engagement, gather customer feedback, and cultivate cultural alignment to ensure you have healthy teams and happy customers. As one of our customers, Director of Managed Services Ryan Heath of Dymin, put it, "The thing about the IT By Design partnership that I really enjoyed and I think is fantastic is the fact that you guys are just as involved in ensuring that the technicians are happy, that they're engaged, that they're not being burnt out."

We give you the tools you need to boost customer and employee retention rates and drive up profitability across your business. Our data-driven tools also incorporate proven performance management strategies. So, for example, when we discussed the importance of having entrepreneurial thinkers on your team, Team GPS can help you transform a low-performing employee into a higher-performing one by using in-depth analytics and providing management solutions from there.

It also includes rewards and accolades to keep your people motivated and happy. That's what it is all about, after all. The platform is designed to encourage a positive work culture, promote your core values, and enable peer-to-peer interaction and gamification. We want to make employees feel good about the work they're doing and help them achieve their goals.

Lastly, many of our MSPs are overwhelmed by their various employee management tools. Team GPS also offers a solution by connecting everything on one platform. It is a one-stop shop for connecting key stakeholders and team members and giving you actionable data to build your community at work.

Learn more and request your demo by visiting itbd. net/team-gps today!

Delivering World-Class Talent for Your Team

One of the biggest issues—and biggest costs—facing any business today is finding and recruiting top tech talent. With Talent Ready to Go by IT By Design, we do the hard part for you by finding and training the top talent and delivering them straight to your business.

We hire and train the most promising talent. Then, we put them through an intensive, sixty-day engineering boot camp. If they meet our standards, they join the team, and we add them to our bench. Our team is made up of highly trained tech talent who are ready to go and serve our customers.

Whether you need a cloud engineer, a cybersecurity expert, or a level two tech, we have the talent you need, ready to be deployed. In comparison, normal staffing agencies will take your hiring intake form, review it, provide you with a job description based on the intake form, advertise the position, begin the search, interview candidates, and make their selections. Normally, this process takes between sixty and ninety days, but sometimes it takes even longer—just to hire one person.

All the while, you are stuck waiting to fill the position; your remaining employees get stretched thin to cover the workload, and your customers are left in the lurch as they get passed between intermediaries. It is far from ideal.

Instead, our customers get access to our talent pool the same day or the next day. You can choose whomever you want and as many employees as you need. We regularly keep between fifty and one hundred engineers on our bench, so there are never any gaps for our customers. We cut your hiring time down to almost nothing, which gives you an edge in whatever your industry may be.

In addition to providing engineers at the ready, we also provide services for smaller customers with one-stop network operations center (NOC) solutions. If you do not need a designated employee or full-time resources team but you only want to build a team of, say, five or ten engineers, then our NOC services might be a better fit for you. This is a great option for MSPs looking to reduce costs, grow revenue, and provide top-tier security to their own customers.

Beyond NOC services, we also offer remote monitoring and management (RMM), security operations centers (SOC) with Shield IT, and professional services with Special IT.

To find your next great engineer, head to <u>itbd.net/services/</u> <u>managed-service-provider-staffing</u>, or to learn more about our other cost-saving, revenue-boosting talent solutions, check out <u>itbd.net/services/network-operations-center-noc</u> and get in touch! We will get started helping you scale your business and improve customer experience.

Build IT Technical and Leadership Training

The final piece of the puzzle is our technical and leadership training services, which we call Build IT. We help our customers train their leaders, technicians, and engineers. We cover a broad range of subjects—everything from an entrepreneurial thinking curriculum to deep dives on the kind of technology stacks to use, how to create positive culture, profit and loss analysis methods, or best practice strategies for hiring and retaining top talent.

We hold regular workshops and conferences for leadership development training. We want to help you bridge the gap between knowledge and success by providing exciting, engaging opportunities for lifelong learning. These are hugely popular, successful events, and they are also a lot of fun. The feedback we get from attendees is so positive.

For instance, "What a great time Sunny and Kam have created for the partners and vendors. Build IT powered by IT By Design was such a hit, and we still have another day! Wonderful meeting some new and old friends!" said Joel Zaidspiner, VP of The ChannelPro Network.

Kevin Brown, a motivational speaker and best-selling author, said, "A world-class event because of world-class people."

Or take what Jayme Branson, CEO of Granite Technology Solutions, had to say after attending, "Thank you, IT By Design, for the best conference ever! I fell in love with the whole team led by Sunny Kaila and Kam Kaila and their heart to share knowledge and help the MSP community become stronger."

Everyone who attends leaves energized and motivated, and they bring that back to their teams. Build IT has three different pillars: Communities of Practice, our corporate trainings; Build IT University for online self-learning courses; and Build It Live, our annual conference. Join the fun and the conversation by visiting itbd.net/live/#.

Final Thoughts on the Journey Ahead

With these three services—Team GPS, MSP staffing and NOC services, and Build IT trainings and conferences—the bases are loaded. It's just up to you to hit the grand slam and bring it all home.

Culture will happen, so it is just a matter of you making a choice: do you want to create that culture by design, or are you going to let it happen by default? Because it is a choice. If you choose to create Culture By Design, then you will be at the wheel. You will be in charge of what your company culture looks like and how your employees and customers experience it. It's a big responsibility—and an unmissable opportunity.

As we know, in the words of Peter Drucker, culture eats strategy for breakfast. Without culture, there is no sustainable success. So, it is important to pay attention and be intentional when it comes to creating culture. If you only do one thing as a leader, focus on your culture, everything else will fall into place.

When you implement the TOS and Life By Design framework, you will attract the best talent, which means you will have an abundance of top talent supporting your vision. You will be surrounded by people who are dedicated to the same vision of success. You can start any project without the worry of having to shoulder all the burdens by yourself. You will have people there to do that work for you and help put out any fires along the way.

If there is only one thing you can do to ensure that you attract top talent, it is to focus on high-pay-off activity. This will give you freedom in so many different areas of your life. If you can earn people, money will follow you. Culture creation is, at its heart, a people strategy. You have to learn how to earn people and take care of them as human beings. And at the end of the day, people are going to do work. But are you willing to do the work, too?

As I have said so many times in this book, culture is a journey. You have to start somewhere. You have to be intentional. Keep developing yourself and your people. It will reward you with good people and positive culture. And, if you can create that vibrant community at work, you will be a successful entrepreneur and a successful leader. You can be a successful manager and a successful supervisor. Take your responsibility towards people seriously, and you will reap the rewards of what you sow for years to come.

I hope that you come away from reading this book with a renewed sense of purpose for yourself, your company, and your team as a whole. I hope that this book has been useful in getting you to think deeply about different solutions to the problems stopping your business from being everything it has the potential to be. And I hope that our paths cross again. I hope we see you on your journey.

Notes

1   Vikram Ahuja. "The War for Talent Is the 'New Normal.'" *Forbes*. 8 July 2022. https://www.forbes.com/sites/forbesbusinesscouncil/2022/07/08/the-war-for-talent-in-the-new-normal/?sh=24e18366689e; Sheryl Estrada. "The war for talent has turned into the 'war for skills.'" *Fortune*. 17 January 2023. https://fortune.com/2023/01/17/war-for-talent-turned-into-war-for-skills/; "Overview 2023: The ever-increasing war for talent." *LinkedIn Pulse*. 7 December 2022.

2   "Talent War Set to Be Top Priority for CIOs in 2023, Study Reveals." *CEO Digital*. 8 September 2022. https://ceo.digital/news/war-for-talent-set-to-increase-2023.

3   "Report: Inflation, Labor Shortages Top HR Concerns in 2023" *Society for Human Resource Management*. 30 January 2023. https://www.shrm.org/hr-today/news/hr-news/pages/report-inflation-labor-shortages-top-hr-concerns-in-2023.aspx

4   RN Bhaskar. "India in the 1980s: The lull that shaped the storm." *Forbes India*. 12 August 2019. https://www.forbesindia.com/article/independence-special-2019/india-in-the-1980s-the-lull-that-shaped-the-storm/54779/1

5   Jonathan Woetzel and Jeongmin Seong. "What is driving Asia's technological rise?" *McKinsey Global Institute*. 5

January 2021. https://www.mckinsey.com/mgi/overview/in-the-news/what-is-driving-asias-technological-rise

6   Oliver Tonby and Jonathan Woetzel. "Asia's technological path to growth." *Financial Times.* https://www.ft.com/partnercontent/mckinsey/asias-technological-path-to-growth.html

7   Suman Bhattacharyya. "Tech Wage Inflation Puts Pressure on Companies." *The Wall Street Journal.* 21 April 2022. https://www.wsj.com/articles/tech-wage-inflation-puts-pressure-on-companies-11650533400

8   Tomas Chamorro-Premuzic and Jonathan Kirschner. "How the Best Managers Identify and Develop Talent." *Harvard Business Review.* 9 January 2020. https://hbr.org/2020/01/how-the-best-managers-identify-and-develop-talent?registration=success

9   Steve Ashby. "The Hidden Cost of Underperforming Employees and Freelancers and What to Do About It." *LinkedIn.* 1 January 2018. https://www.linkedin.com/pulse/hidden-cost-underperforming-employees-freelancers-nd-what-steve-ashby/

10   Ibid.

11   Eric Garton. "The Case for Investing More in People." *Harvard Business Review.* 4 Sept. 2017. https://hbr.org/2017/09/the-case-for-investing-more-in-people

12   Eric Garton and Michael C. Mankins. *Time, Talent, Energy: Overcome Organizational Drag and Unleash Your Team's Productive Power.* Harvard Business Review Press. 2017.

13   "Our Culture." *Four Seasons.* Accessed: 1 May 2023. *https://www.fourseasons.com/landing-pages/corporate/careers/our-culture/*

14   Tracy Francis and Fernanda Hoefel. "'True Gen': Generation Z and its implications for companies." *McKinsey & Company.* 12 November 2018. https://www.mckinsey.

com/industries/consumer-packaged-goods/our-insights/
true-gen-generation-z-and-its-implications-for-companies

15   Ibid.

16   "Generation Influence: Gen Z Study Reveals a New
     Digital Paradigm." *Business Wire.* 7 July 2020. https://
     www.businesswire.com/news/home/20200706005543/en/
     Generation-Influence-Gen-Z-Study-Reveals-a-New-
     Digital-Paradigm

17   Dangmei, Jianguanglung & Singh, Amarendra.
     "Understanding the Generation Z: The Future Workforce."
     South-Asian Journal of Multidisciplinary Studies. Vol. 3:3.
     1-5. 2016.

18   "Is MrBeast actually worth $1.5 billion?" *Tech Crunch.*
     25 October 2022. https://techcrunch.com/2022/10/25/
     mrbeast-1-5-billion-valuation-youtuber/

19   "Profile: Jimmy Donaldson (Mr. Beast)." *Forbes.*
     Accessed 3 May 2023. https://www.forbes.com/profile/
     jimmy-donaldson-mrbeast/

20   Dan Schwabel (2014) as cited in Dangmei, Jianguanglung &
     Singh, Amarendra. "Understanding the Generation Z: The
     Future Workforce." *South-Asian Journal of Multidisciplinary
     Studies.* Vol. 3:3. 1-5. 2016.

21   Katie Navarra. "The Real Costs of Recruitment." *Society for
     Human Resource Management.* 11 April 2022. https://www.
     shrm.org/resourcesandtools/hr-topics/talent-acquisition/
     pages/the-real-costs-of-recruitment.aspx

22   Peter Cappelli. "Your Approach to Hiring Is All Wrong."
     Harvard Business Review. May-June 2019. https://hbr.
     org/2019/05/your-approach-to-hiring-is-all-wrong

23   Katie Navarra. "The Real Costs of Recruitment." *Society for
     Human Resource Management.* 11 April 2022. https://www.
     shrm.org/resourcesandtools/hr-topics/talent-acquisition/
     pages/the-real-costs-of-recruitment.aspx

Acknowledgments

Thanks to the entire IT By Design community for their positive impact on this world. I appreciate all of those individuals who supported me in achieving my Life By Design vision. No team, no American Dream!

About Sunny Kaila

Sunny Kaila is the Founder, CEO, and real-life American Dream behind IT By Design, the leading talent solutions provider for MSPs across the globe. Sunny sees opportunities where others see hurdles and isn't afraid to embrace thoughtful risk when the time comes to take a leap of faith. That mindset has turned Sunny's early 2000s step into the world of entrepreneurship into a global company with over 600 employees across five facilities, servicing small and mid-sized companies across various industries.

He authentically shares his journey as an immigrant from India and his rise to success in the tech industry through speaking engagements, writings, and his podcast, Sunny's Silver Linings. His empowering keynote, Talentpreneurship: How to Build and Grow a Healthy Business, Transform the People Around You, and Live the Life of Your Dreams, continues to resonate with audiences worldwide.

Sunny has received various humanitarian and industry awards based on his community service for his impact. He lives in New Jersey with his wonderful wife, Kam Kaila, and three boys.

Connect with Sunny at Talentpreneurship.net

LEARN HOW TO FIND TRAINED TALENT... AND KEEP THEM.

Sunny Kaila Will Show You How.

KEYNOTE SPEAKER

START THE CONVERSATION TODAY

ITBD.NET

CONNECT WITH SUNNY

Follow him on your favorite social media platforms today.

ITBD.NET

TALENT, TRAINING & TOOLS
FOR MSPs WHO WANT MORE PROFITS & MORE STABILITY

ITBD.NET

THIS BOOK IS PROTECTED INTELLECTUAL PROPERTY

The author of this book values Intellectual Property. The book you just read is protected by Easy IP™, a proprietary process, which integrates blockchain technology giving Intellectual Property "Global Protection." By creating a "Time-Stamped" smart contract that can never be tampered with or changed, we establish "First Use" that tracks back to the author.

Easy IP™ functions much like a Pre-Patent™ since it provides an immutable "First Use" of the Intellectual Property. This is achieved through our proprietary process of leveraging blockchain technology and smart contracts. As a result, proving "First Use" is simple through a global and verifiable smart contract. By protecting intellectual property with blockchain technology and smart contracts, we establish a "First to File" event.

Powered By Easy IP™

LEARN MORE AT EASYIP.TODAY

Made in the USA
Columbia, SC
26 August 2023

22087934R00096